RAND NATIONAL DEFENSE RESEARCH INSTITUTE

T0146382

A Framework for Programming and Budgeting for Cybersecurity

John S. Davis II, Martin C. Libicki, Stuart E. Johnson,
Jason Kumar, Michael Watson, Andrew Karode

Prepared for the Department of Homeland Security

For more information on this publication, visit www.rand.org/t/TL186

Library of Congress Cataloging-in-Publication Data is available for this publication.
ISBN: 978-0-8330-9256-4

Published by the RAND Corporation, Santa Monica, Calif.

© Copyright 2016 RAND Corporation

RAND® is a registered trademark.

www.rand.org

Preface

The U.S. Department of Homeland Security (DHS) has primary responsibility for the security of the nation's unclassified cyber networks. To function, the nation's economy and government have become increasingly dependent on reliable and secure networks, making this mission increasingly critical.

This study examines the capabilities presented in the DHS report *Blueprint for a Secure Cyber Future* and how these capabilities fit in within the context of broad set of cybersecurity activities that can be used to defend a network. This study recommends an approach to evaluating cybersecurity defensive activities.

The study was sponsored by Program, Analysis, and Evaluation (PA&E) of the Office of the Chief Financial Officer, DHS. It will be of interest to policymakers and program managers who have responsibility for cybersecurity, particularly of the nation's unclassified networks.

This study builds on a broad set of studies that RAND has done in the fields of cybersecurity and of program analysis.

The RAND Homeland Security and Defense Center

The research reported here was conducted in the Homeland Security and Defense Center (HSDC), which conducts analysis to prepare and protect communities and critical infrastructure from natural disasters and terrorism. Center projects examine a wide range of risk-management problems, including coastal and border security, emergency preparedness and response, defense support to civil authorities, transportation security, domestic intelligence, and technology acquisition. Center clients include the U.S. Department of Homeland Security, the U.S. Department of Defense, the U.S. Department of Justice, and other organizations charged with security and disaster preparedness, response, and recovery.

HSDC is a joint center of two research divisions: RAND Justice, Infrastructure, and Environment and the RAND National Security Research Division. RAND Justice, Infrastructure, and Environment is dedicated to improving policy and decisionmaking in a wide range of policy domains, including civil and criminal justice, infrastructure protection and homeland security, transportation and energy policy, and environmental and natural resource policy. The RAND National Security Research Division conducts research and analysis for all national security sponsors other than the U.S. Air Force and the Army. The division includes the National Defense Research Institute, a federally funded research and development center whose sponsors include the Office of the Secretary of Defense, the Joint Staff, the Unified Combatant Commands, the defense agencies, and the U.S. Department of the Navy. The National Security Research Division also conducts research for the U.S. intelligence community and the ministries of defense of U.S. allies and partners.

Contents

Figures

Summary

In cyberspace, hacker attacks can draw from many options, and the defender must be prepared to respond to all possible attacks. These defensive preparations and responses cover a wide range of possibilities. Each activity, when taken individually, is often tractable and, in some cases, is easy to execute. Nevertheless, the activities incur a cost, and no single activity (or subset of activities) is sufficient to guarantee security within cyberspace. Hence, the cybersecurity professional is faced with the dilemma of selecting an appropriate set of cybersecurity defensive measures from a vast array of options, and this selection process occurs for most, if not all, professionals while operating with a limited set of resources to employ the measures.

This dilemma is faced in both the private and public sectors, including in the U.S. Department of Homeland Security (DHS). In 2011, DHS leadership directed a broad, department-wide review of the challenges it faced in implementing its charter to secure the nation's non-defense networks. The resultant report,[1] *Blueprint for a Secure Cyber Future*, outlines the challenges posed by hostile actors, operator error, and faulty software design, among others. The DHS Blueprint identifies 75 capabilities (25 of them "critical") that would enhance the security of the nation's networks.

A challenge in using the DHS Blueprint as a framework for programming and budgeting is that the capabilities are presented as an itemized list. This leads to several difficulties:

- *Lack of Inter-Capability Relationships*: It is difficult to determine from the DHS Blueprint how any two capabilities may depend on or influence each other.
- *Lack of Prioritization*: Beyond its distinction between priority and nonpriority capabilities, the DHS Blueprint offers no mechanism for prioritizing the importance of the capabilities.
- *Missing Influences*: The DHS Blueprint attempts to present a comprehensive list of capabilities, but the roles and the influences of other noncapability activities are not captured.

In this report, we aim to address these difficulties and help explain the menu of actions for defending an organization against cyberattack. We present of set of over 100 actions that can serve as elements of a cyberdefense strategy, and we support the selection process by identifying the interrelationships among the activities. This approach provides a basis by which the practitioner can allocate and prioritize activities according to dependencies between the activities. Our approach is in contrast to typical cybersecurity guides, in which a set of activities is

---

[1] U.S. Department of Homeland Security, *Blueprint for a Secure Cyber Future: The Cybersecurity Strategy for the Homeland Security Enterprise*, Washington, D.C., 2014.

presented within sequential lists that do not emphasize dependencies—or cost-effectiveness, for that matter.[2]

We organize the relationships via hierarchical decomposition. This decomposition process presumes that any two activities that are directly related can be characterized as having a parent-child relationship. In our presentation, a parent-child link represents one of two types of relationships: composition or requisition. In a composition relationship, the parent (or general) activity is an aggregation of two or more child (or specific) activities (e.g., a meal can be modeled as a parent activity that is composed of a salad activity, an appetizer activity, an entrée activity, and a dessert activity). In a requisition relationship, one or more child (specific) activities must be completed (are *required*) before the parent (or general) activity can take place (e.g., a meal can be modeled as a parent activity that can only occur after the activities of buying, cooking, and serving food have occurred). The distinction between composite and requisite hierarchy can be applied on an as-needed basis, and may depend on the reader's interpretation of a set of activities; we raise the distinction principally to allow for a flexible hierarchical model. Inherent in our hierarchical decomposition is the notion that all child activities have a single parent activity; in practice, this assumption does not hold in the context of cybersecurity, but for the purposes of our exposition, such a constraint is not particularly limiting.

A hierarchical decomposition approach lends itself to representation in many ways. We chose a sunburst graph in order to place the overarching goal at the center of the graph and the various actions are successively at further remove from the center. Furthermore, the chart displays not only vertical relationships (parent-child) but relationships across branches. The sunburst chart results in a ringed representation. Ring 0 (the center of the chart) contains our overarching goal of reducing expected cost of cyberattacks.[3] Ring 1 consists of strategies that support ring 0, and, more generally, ring N+1 supports ring N. An illustration of the cyber sunburst graph is displayed in Figure S.1.[4]

The relative importance of each action is indicated by the magnitude of the angle of the given action's wedge with respect to peer actions. In the case of the four top-level strategies, "neutralize attacks" is allocated an angle of 180 degrees, "accelerate recovery" is allocated an angle of 40 degrees, and "minimize exposure" and "increase resilience" are both allocated an angle of 70 degrees. These angles are intended to serve as approximations of relative importance with a nod to prioritization more so than precise allocation of resources (e.g., "neutralize attacks" is more important than "increase resilience," which, in turn, is more important than "minimize exposure").

Our set of cyberdefense actions and the corresponding relationships were derived initially as hypotheses based on the authors' cyber experiences in conjunction with relevant literature review. Subsequently, an iterative process involving third-party expert review was used to refine the enumerations and relationships. The relationships and angles we present throughout this report are meant to be illustrative; valid approaches to specifying these could be developed through one of multiple approaches (such as empirical evaluation of incident data with a specific system, domain expert elicitation, or analysis of budgets). The value of this approach lies

[2]   U.S. Department of Commerce, National Institute of Standards and Technology, *Security and Privacy Controls for Federal Information Systems and Organizations*, Special Publication 800-53, 2013; U.S. Department of Energy, *21 Steps to Improve Cyber Security of SCADA Networks*, 2009.

[3]   We assume that the cost of cyberattacks is minimized within the context of utilizing software that is best suited for the enterprise at hand.

[4]   Extensive digital rendering of the sunburst diagram falls out of scope of this work. The graph's contents are detailed in Chapters Three and Four.

Figure S.1
The Cyber Sunburst Graph

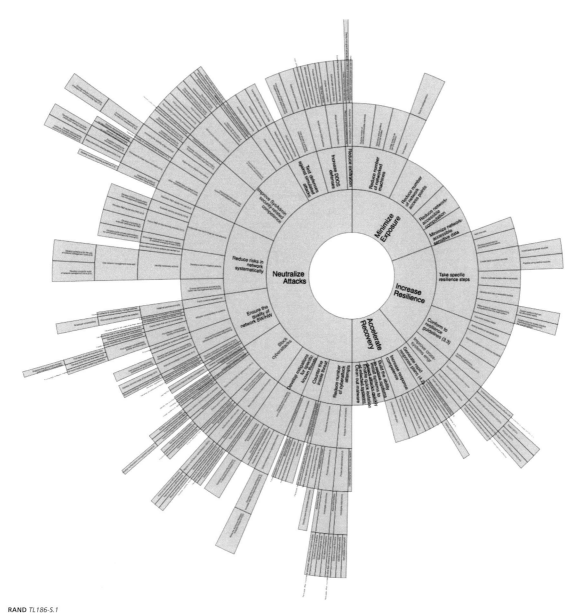

not in the precision of the outcome but rather the general shape of the graph of activities. Furthermore, the prioritization implied by our depiction of the strategies is distinct from the process of assigning actions to the strategies. Any given cybersecurity specialist may quibble with the details at the margins of our chart, but application of this approach will still provide useful insight.

It should be noted that, in aggregate, the presented actions are of value to many different communities. Some actions are more relevant to CISOs (chief information security officers) employed in corporate settings, while other actions have relevance to policymakers operating within the federal government. We believe the contents of this report will be of interest to both public- and private-sector professionals involved in setting policies and creating strategies for ensuring cybersecurity.

Acknowledgments

The authors would first like to thank our Department of Homeland Security liaisons, Dana Fronczak and Aldo Prosperi, who made this research possible and provided useful input as the work progressed. We are also grateful to the experienced RAND cyber professionals who provided valuable insights as we engaged in our research and developed our methodology. These cyber professionals included Lily Ablon, Igor Mikolic-Torreira, and Tim Webb. Finally, we would like to thank our RAND reviewers, Sasha Romanosky, David Senty, Cynthia Cook, and Laura Baldwin, whose feedback significantly improved our report.

Abbreviations

API	application programmer interface
CISO	chief information security officer
CISSP	Certified Information Systems Security Professional
CNCI	Comprehensive National Cybersecurity Initiative
DDOS	distributed denial of service
DHS	U.S. Department of Homeland Security
DHS CFO/PA&E	U.S. Department of Homeland Security Chief Financial Officer/Program Analysis and Evaluation
FBI	Federal Bureau of Investigation
FTP	file transfer protocol
IDS/IPS	intrusion detection system/intrusion prevention system
INFOCON	information operation condition
IP	Internet Protocol
ISAC	Information Sharing and Analysis Center
IT	information technology
MFA	multifactor authentication
NIST	National Institute of Standards and Technology
NSA	National Security Agency
NSTIC	National Strategy for Trusted Identity in Cyberspace
NTP	Network Time Protocol
PIN	Personal Identification Number
R&D	research and development
SCADA	Supervisory Control And Data Acquisition
SPOF	single point of failure

CHAPTER ONE

Motivation

Cyberwar enthusiasts (and cyberdefense pessimists) like quoting the warning given by a member of the Irish Republican Army after failing to assassinate Prime Minister Margaret Thatcher at the Grand Hotel in Brighton: "Today we were unlucky, but remember we only have to be lucky once. You will have to be lucky always."[1] This warning is not only applicable to cybersecurity but, from the defender's perspective, is arguably more acute in a cyber context than in the physical domain. Cyberspace and the computing systems therein have several characteristics that make them more susceptible to attack vis-à-vis their physical counterparts. First, computing systems are highly connected, providing would-be attackers with many points of access. Second, computing systems are so complex (notably in their component integration) that many points of access are unknown to their owners. Third (and perhaps most importantly), computing systems are dynamic and constantly changing, with new installations and application upgrades that compound the connectedness and complexity. A cybersecurity professional can never rest.

The result is that in cyberspace, hacker attacks can draw from many options, and the defender must be prepared to respond to all possible attacks. Consider the cyberattack against Home Depot that was made public in September 2014, in which multiple attack points were used to gain malicious access, including stolen vendor credentials, exploitation of a Microsoft operating system vulnerability, the compromise of the company's point-of-sale systems, and control of the self-checkout computer systems.[2] The defensive preparations and responses necessary to avoid such an attack cover a wide range of possibilities and include keeping software systems updated to minimize vulnerabilities, installing effective tools for intercepting known attack types, encouraging employees and vendors to use appropriate passwords and educating them to avoid social engineering, and logging activity to facilitate post-incident forensics. Each activity, when taken individually, is often tractable and, in some cases, is easy to execute. Nevertheless, the activities incur a cost, and no single activity (or subset of activities) is sufficient to guarantee security within cyberspace.

Given that most, if not all, organizations operate with limited resources, the prospect of executing all activities is unrealistic (and even overwhelming), and in practice many chief information security officers (CISOs) think that the cost of carrying out multiple security actions rises nonlinearly. Hence, the cybersecurity professional is faced with the dilemma of selecting a set of cybersecurity defensive measures, the sum total of which must be chosen

---

[1] David Hughes, "Brighton Bombing: Daily Telegraph Journalist Recalls," *The Telegraph*, October 11, 2009.

[2] Shelly Banjo, "Home Depot Hackers Exposed 53 Million Email Addresses," *Wall Street Journal*, November 6, 2015.

1

based on practicality more so than optimality. Choosing among this large set of possibilities is not easy.

As the federal agency with the responsibility of securing the nation's nondefense cyber networks, the U.S. Department of Homeland Security (DHS) also faces this stark challenge of developing and recommending a cyberdefense strategy. The challenge is especially daunting for DHS given that the networks, which DHS must influence, are largely owned and operated by private corporations. DHS does not have the authority to mandate standards, so it must rely largely on providing a recommendation that encourages the providers to conform to effective security standards in particular and best practices more generally. This is not to say that DHS cannot have a useful influence on securing the nation's networks. It has resources ($38.2 billion in the President's Budget for fiscal year 2015), a growing research and development (R&D) program, and control of gateway services for a widely used network that it manages (the .gov domain).

In 2011, DHS leadership directed a broad, department-wide review of the challenges it faced in implementing its charter to secure the nation's non-defense networks. The resultant report, *Blueprint for a Secure Cyber Future*, outlines the challenges posed by hostile actors, operator error, and faulty software design, among others.[3] The DHS Blueprint identifies 75 capabilities (25 of them "critical") that would enhance the security of the nations' networks.

In a preceding study prepared for the DHS Security Chief Financial Officer/Program Analysis and Evaluation (DHS CFO/PA&E) (and which is not publicly available), RAND reviewed the DHS Blueprint findings. A key conclusion was that, while the document contained a great number of useful insights, it did not provide an analytic framework for the DHS CFO/PA&E staff to make decisions on how to allocate constrained resources among competing programs to ensure the greatest impact. A challenge in using the DHS Blueprint as a framework for programming and budgeting is that the capabilities are presented as an itemized list. This leads to several difficulties:

- *Lack of Inter-Capability Relationships:* It is difficult to determine from the DHS Blueprint how any two capabilities may depend on or influence each other.
- *Lack of Prioritization:* Beyond the distinction between priority and nonpriority capabilities, the DHS Blueprint offers no mechanism for prioritizing the importance of the capabilities.
- *Missing Influences:* The DHS Blueprint attempts to present a comprehensive list of capabilities, but the roles and the influences of other noncapability activities are not captured.

Given the above backdrop, the aim of this report is to provide a method that organizations can use for addressing these difficulties and to help explain the menu of actions for defending an organization against cyberattack.

That noted, no organization should plunge into this approach without prior reflection about what its needs to defend and how badly. For instance, if I have information on my network, what can I afford to lose and what can I not afford to lose? What are the consequences of my losing it—is my reputation at stake, my ability to be first to market with new products, the privacy of my employees? Who might be interested in it? Why? How badly? How

---

[3] U.S. Department of Homeland Security, *Blueprint for a Secure Cyber Future: The Cybersecurity Strategy for the Homeland Security Enterprise*, Washington, D.C., 2014.

much risk would they be willing to take to get it? If I have operations to carry out, how time-critical are they, and how will security procedures impact achieving these deadlines? How much flexibility do I have to adjust operations? What is my legal or contractual liability if operations are stopped? Who might be interested in stopping such operations? An understanding of security risks and the procedures necessary to minimize these risks is the *sine qua non* of cybersecurity—it cannot be overemphasized. Only *after* such questions have been asked can organizations determine what needs to be protected, how, and with what tools.

CHAPTER TWO

Core Concepts

In this report, we present of set of over 100 actions that can serve as elements of a cyberdefense strategy. As implied above, not all activities need be employed, and not all are equally important; any organization responsible for managing a secure computing system must pick and choose. We believe that an important facility necessary to support the selection process is to consider the interrelationships among the activities. The key point here is that cybersecurity activities are difficult to assess in isolation, because the execution of any given activity will affect the efficacy of some set of other activities. Our approach provides a basis by which the practitioner can allocate and prioritize activities according to dependencies between the activities. Our approach is in contrast to typical cybersecurity guides, in which a set of activities is presented within sequential lists that do not emphasize dependencies—or cost-effectiveness, for that matter.[1]

We organize the relationships via hierarchical decomposition. This decomposition process presumes that any two activities that are directly related can be characterized as having a parent-child relationship. In our presentation, a parent-child link represents one of two types of relationships: composition or requisition. In a composition relationship, the parent (or general) activity is an aggregation of two or more child (or specific) activities (e.g., a meal can be modeled as a parent activity that is composed of a salad activity, an appetizer activity, an entrée activity, and a dessert activity). In a requisition relationship, one or more child (specific) activities must be completed (are *required*) before the parent (or general) activity can take place (e.g., a meal can be modeled as a parent activity that can only occur after the activities of buying, cooking, and serving food have occurred). The distinction between composite and requisite hierarchy can be applied on an as-needed basis, and may depend on the reader's interpretation of a set of activities; we raise the distinction principally to allow for a flexible hierarchical model. Inherent in our hierarchical decomposition is the notion that all child activities have a single parent activity; in practice, this assumption does not hold in the context of cybersecurity, but for the purposes of our exposition, such a constraint is not particularly limiting.

It should be noted that there are general actions whose combined specific actions constitute only a fraction of what is required to carry out the general action. By way of illustration, consider the general action "drive to Atlanta." Prerequisite specific actions may be to pack the car, gas it up, and grab a map—but that still leaves the actual driving, something that might

---

[1] U.S. Department of Commerce, National Institute of Standards and Technology, *Security and Privacy Controls for Federal Information Systems and Organizations*, Special Publication 800-53, 2013; U.S. Department of Energy, *21 Steps to Improve Cyber Security of SCADA Networks*, 2009.

not be meaningfully reduced to components. In what follows, one will see general actions whose realization is more than the sum of their prerequisites or components.

A hierarchical decomposition approach lends itself to representation in many ways. We chose a sunburst graph in order to place the overarching goal at the center of the graph and the various actions successively farther from the center. Furthermore, the chart displays not only vertical relationships (parent-child) but relationships across branches. The sunburst chart results in a ringed representation. Ring 0 (the center of the chart) contains our overarching goal of reducing the expected cost of cyberattacks.[2] Ring 1 consists of strategies that support ring 0, and, more generally, ring N+1 supports ring N. An illustration of the Cyber Sunburst Graph is displayed in Figure 2.1.[3]

The relative importance of each action is indicated by the angle of the given action's wedge with respect to peer actions (other children of a common parent action). Wedges with larger angles are considered more important than wedges on the same ring with smaller angles; for example, as shown in Figure 2.2, "neutralize attacks" has a larger angle than "increase resilience" and therefore is considered a more important defensive strategy. The angles provide a basis for allocation of resources across a set of cybersecurity actions under consideration and are easily represented in a sunburst diagram. The angles shown in the figures that follow are intended to serve as approximations of relative importance with a nod to prioritization more so than precision.

Our set of cyberdefense actions and the corresponding relationships were derived initially as hypotheses based on the authors' cyber experiences in conjunction with relevant literature review.[4] Subsequently, an iterative process involving third-party review was used to refine the enumerations and relationships. The value of this approach lies not in the precision of the outcome but rather in the underlying logic of the structure and interconnections of cyberdefensive activities. Any given cybersecurity specialist may quibble with the details at the margins of our chart (and some of the quibbling may be sector-dependent), but application of this approach will still provide useful insight. More importantly, our approach does not depend on the *specific list of actions* presented in the subsequent sections of this report, or on the relative size of the actions. The actions we present throughout this report are meant to be illustrative; valid approaches to specifying these could be developed through one of multiple approaches (such as empirical evaluation of incident data with a specific system, domain expert elicitation, or analysis of budgets). We believe that the principal contribution of this work is not the identification of a specific enumeration of actions but the recognition that cyberdefensive actions are interrelated and that some actions should take precedence over others. Our approach enables a prioritization process that is much needed by the overburdened cybersecurity practitioner. Indeed, this approach can be applied to other domains unrelated to cybersecurity that involve complex compliance processes.

It should be noted that, in aggregate, the cyberdefensive actions that we present are of value to many different communities. Some actions are more relevant to CISOs employed in corporate settings, while other actions have relevance to policymakers operating within the

---

[2]   We assume that the cost of cyberattacks is minimized within the context of utilizing software that is best suited for the enterprise at hand.

[3]   Extensive digital rendering of the sunburst diagram falls out of scope of this work. The graph's contents are detailed in Chapters Three and Four.

[4]   A subset of the actions includes capabilities from the DHS Blueprint and these actions are indicated as applicable.

Figure 2.1
The Cyber Sunburst Graph

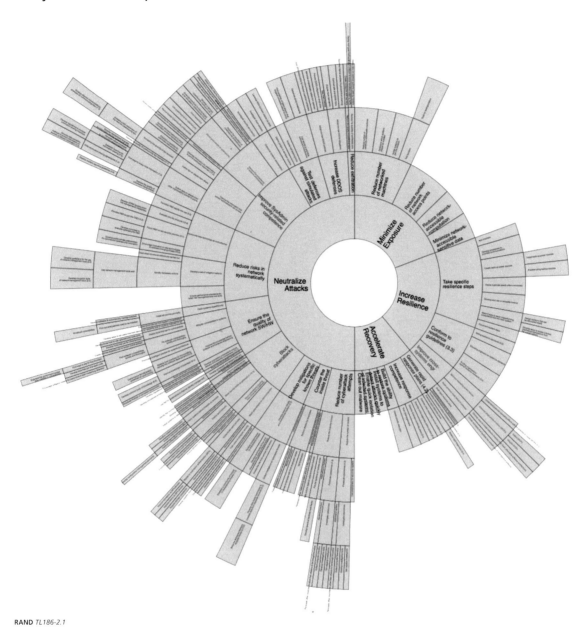

federal government. We believe the strategies and actions presented in this report will be of interest to both public- and private-sector professionals involved in setting policies and creating strategies for ensuring cybersecurity.

Goal: Reduce the Expected Cost of Cyberattacks

We posit that cybersecurity has an overarching goal: a reduction in the expected cost of cyber-attacks. Several assumptions are packed into this goal. First, we use cost to mean impact,

Figure 2.2
The Four Basic Strategies

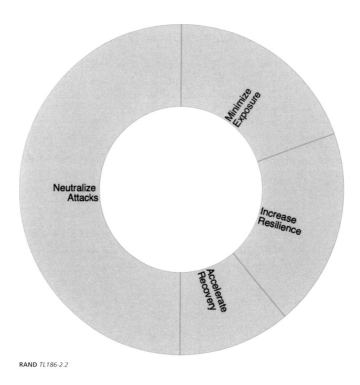

RAND *TL186-2.2*

expressed in a quasi-monetized way; in some cases, a cyberattack leads to an explicit monetary cost involving labor and/or computing resources, while in other cases the cost is less tangible (e.g., a military impact may not necessarily be reduced to dollars and cents). In truth, many of these risks, even for businesses, are hard to capture. Organizations look at lost reputation as a cost. Nations might measure reduced personal privacy or increased risks to national security. Second, we use "expected" costs to include the risk of low-likelihood, high-impact events, such as a cyberattack on the power grid or a military defeat. These stand in contrast to day-to-day costs arising from more common cyberattacks, such as cybercrimes. Third, many of the costs of even those cyberattacks that have already occurred are unknown and, today, unknowable. If a U.S. firm has had its intellectual property stolen (e.g., by the Chinese), its share of global markets might not be reduced by competition from Chinese copycat products until years later, if then. We recognize that cyberattacks can have many effects. Some affect confidentiality; others affect integrity; still others affect availability.[5]

Many of the actions called for below may not pertain to all three types of attacks. Recovery and resiliency actions, to note two responses, are much more relevant to attacks on availability (e.g., a power outage) than to attacks on confidentiality (many of which are not discovered until after the fact) or integrity (similarly). Finally, we assume that reducing the expected cost of cyberattacks occurs within the context of utilizing the software that is best suited for the enterprise at hand; we presume that users desire to bring cyberattack costs down while still taking advantage of the benefits of modern technology.

---

[5]   Chad Perrin, "The CIA Triad," TechRepublic.com blog, June 30, 2008.

Ring 1: Four Basic Strategies

Our set of actions are categorized into four basic strategies that support the goal of reducing the expected costs of cyberattack, as illustrated:

- Minimize exposure.
- Neutralize attacks.
- Increase resilience.
- Accelerate recovery.

Although the four are intended to be both complete and distinct, in practice there is overlap. For instance, although resilience limits the damage of an attack and recovery limits the duration of the damage, some actions, such as instant recovery, might be considered part of both. As shown in the angles of four top-level strategies in Figure 2.2, "neutralize attacks" is allocated an angle of 180 degrees, "accelerate recovery" is allocated an angle of 40 degrees, and "minimize exposure" and "increase resilience" are both allocated an angle of 70 degrees. These angles are intended to serve as approximations of relative importance with a nod to prioritization more so than precise allocation of resources (i.e., "neutralize attacks" is more important than "accelerate recovery"). Thumbnail definitions of the strategies follow:

- *Minimize exposure:* Systems are vulnerable to the extent that others can access them, and their data can be accessed or corrupted only to the extent that such data exists on the system.[6] This action has two components: reducing the linkages between a system and the rest of the world (including the access of insiders to elements of the system), and reducing the information and computational processes (e.g., software programs and executables) that are accessible via the system. In some cases, the severing of internal links within a system can limit the damage from an attack by making it difficult for one subverted node in a network to subvert others.
- *Neutralize attacks:* This, too, is a twofold action: to prevent as many attacks as possible from taking place and to reduce the impact of those attacks that do take place. This duality roughly corresponds to a division of labor between those capabilities that prevent an infection from gaining hold and those that defeat an infection once it *does* gain hold.
- *Increase resilience:* Resilience is related to the ability to carry on the broader functions of an organization even though systems are degraded.[7] It arises from a combination of redundancy and the ability to forego certain support functions without much short-term alteration to higher-level functions (e.g., by rearranging schedules). It also exists in the ability to manage local failures before they become systemic ones. Resilience tends to cover gaps in the short term (the ability to overcome shortfalls permanently without their being recovered does raise the question of why the attacked capability was needed at all).
- *Accelerate recovery:* Recovery applies to the systems being attacked (rather than the functions they support); it operates through repair and substitution.[8] It applies to attacks on

---

[6] Robert Lemos, "NSA Attempting to Design Crack-Proof Computer," *ZDNet.com*, February 1, 2001.

[7] Kishor S. Trivedi, Dong Seong Kim, and Rahul Ghosh, "Resilience in Computer Systems and Networks," presented at 2009 IEEE/ACM International Conference on Computer-Aided Design Digest of Technical Papers, November 2009.

[8] Cisco Systems, Inc., "Disaster Recovery: Best Practices," white paper, 2008.

availability but may be relevant to corruption (to recover the originally correct data or processes) and, to a lesser extent, confidentiality (to recover the former confidence that data is secured).

Note that all four actions have to be taken by or at least on behalf of the organizations under attack or threat of attack. The government is limited in its power to execute any of the four, although, as described at many points below, it is capable of supporting or, in some cases, mandating specific actions that enable these general actions.

The Basis of Our Approach

Our approach is based on the strategy-to-task decomposition methodology as developed at RAND in the late 1980s. The strategy-to-task framework provides a link between broad objectives (strategies) and operational activities (tasks) at the tactical engagement level. The framework explicitly disaggregates the activities into functional tasks that enable the successful execution of the strategy, and it emphasizes the interrelationships among the tasks. Furthermore, the strategy-to-task framework employs hierarchy so that each task can be subsequently disaggregated into subtasks.

The strategy-to-task framework was initially developed for use by the U.S. Air Force.[9] In that context, an example objective might be to deter North Korea from attacking South Korea through the strategy of maintaining a strong forward military presence. By applying the strategy-to-task framework, one recognizes that the objective deterring North Korea consists of two supporting objectives: (1) maintaining a strong forward military presence and (2) isolating North Korea diplomatically. These supporting objectives can be further disaggregated into subordinate activities through a cascading process that results in a hierarchy.

The work in this report applies the strategy-to-task framework to the domain of cybersecurity and extends the framework by leveraging sunburst diagrams to improve visualization. Readers who are interested in more details about the strategy-to-task methodology are directed to publications by Kent and Ochmanek[10] and Thaler.[11]

The Benefits of Our Approach

Before proceeding with an elaboration of the actions that fall under the four strategies, it is worth noting the benefits of our approach. Essentially, we are presenting a large set of possible cyberdefensive actions within a tree structure, and, more specifically, we are presenting the tree via a sunburst diagram (as shown in Figure 2.1). The use of a tree structure facilitates evaluating the actions in a prioritized fashion, with priorities existing at the "top" of the tree (though it should be stated that our work does not necessarily impose a basis for the prioritization). By

---

[9]   David E. Thaler, *Strategies to Tasks: A Framework for Linking Means and Ends*, Santa Monica, Calif.: RAND Corporation, MR-300-AF, 1993.

[10]   Glenn A. Kent and David Ochmanek, *A Framework for Modernization Within the United States Air Force*, Santa Monica, Calif.: RAND Corporation, MR-1706-AF, 2003.

[11]   Thaler, 1993.

displaying the tree as a sunburst diagram, a given prioritization is easily conveyed graphically both in a top-down and peer-wise sense.

These benefits can be expanded with the use of digital tools for rendering the graphical representation.[12] For example, a digital rendering can use color-coding to highlight groups of actions based on similar characteristics. Such renderings and visualization methods help minimize the complexity associated with the large set of cyber actions and may enable easy consumption by cyber practitioners. In Chapter Five of this report, we offer additional ways in which this approach can be used.

---

[12] While extensive digital rendering of the sunburst diagram falls out of scope of this work, we have experimented with and found value in simple tools that illustrate how actions can be (de-)emphasized with automated color highlighting.

CHAPTER THREE

Ring 2

All ring 1 general actions are, in turn, supported by a variety of more specific ring 2 actions. We consider each in turn, starting with the action of reducing unneeded exposure.

Ring 2: Minimize Exposure

We can organize the strategy of reducing unneeded exposure by considering the classes of physical and virtual assets that are subject to access (attack):

- Reduce the number of networked machines.
- Reduce the number of network access points on networked machines.
- Reduce the amount of computational resources on networked machines.
- Minimize the amount of sensitive data on networked machines.

This portion of the Cyber Sunburst Graph is shown in Figure 3.1. As with the other strategies, many of these actions have the potential to impact an organization's productivity. Hence, the associated trade-offs should be considered.

Figure 3.1
The "Minimize Exposure" Strategy with Actions

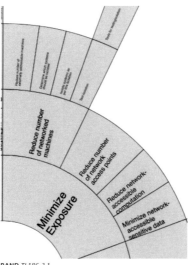

RAND *TL186-3.1*

Reduce the number of networked machines: The fewer the devices that can be addressed via the Internet, the smaller the attack surface of an organization. Alternatives include making such devices local to a particular machine (e.g., a printer that connects only to one computer) or, more generally, making them locally rather than globally accessible. Machines that contain especially sensitive assets should be considered for air-gapping. An air-gapped system is one not connected in real-time to the Internet and/or phone system (or to other systems so connected). Strictly air-gapped systems are those without intermittent connection (e.g., via thumb drives) and close-in communications (e.g., via Bluetooth, Wi-Fi). CISOs talk about achieving the same level of security with virtual air-gapping (e.g., connections among two systems which communicate encrypted traffic across the Internet), but virtual air-gapping is only as safe as the requisite protocols are secure.

Reduce the number of network access points on networked machines: Network-accessible computers contain several resources (virtual ports, applications, services) that can provide external access. Examples include file transfer protocol (FTP) ports and web application servers. This activity entails limiting these points of access. A counterexample is a networked printer exposed to the Internet with all of its ports open (e.g., an outsider can Telnet into it). A variation on this activity involves using nonstandard ports for important network applications (configuring SSH [Secure Shell] with a TCP [Transmission Control Protocol] port other than 22, for instance).

Reduce the amount of computational resources on networked machines: When an external actor gains access to a computer node, that node's computational resources become access points through which a hacker's reach can be extended. Any process available for exploitation on a commandeered machine is a potential risk. The fewer the number processes that can be exploited and legal commands that can be exchanged among machines, the harder it is to mount an external (or internal) attack on a machine, and the more difficult it is to use the infected machine as a platform to infect others. A related tactic is to reduce the physical computational resources (e.g., processors, memory) on exploitable machines. Thin-client machines do less internal processing than desktop machines typically do. For example, many organizations are replacing desktop machines with tablet computers where the additional resources and costs are unnecessary; as a side effect, the corresponding cybersecurity risks are lessened. This reduces their attack surface, which can be quite helpful against attacks that exploit weaknesses in client-side software (e.g., Java, ".pdf" readers) to achieve a foothold in organizations. These actions come under the well-known cybersecurity principle of "least privilege" which states that at any given time, each user or process in a computer system should be able to access only the information and resources that are essential to that user's work.[1]

Minimize the amount of sensitive data on networked machines: Sensitive data includes personally identifiable information as well as strategic organizational information that would pose a threat if unwarranted access were gained. Minimizing exposure can be achieved by placing such data on machines that are more isolated from the Internet (and from potentially rogue insiders) than they otherwise would be. It can also be done by not collecting (or collecting but not digitizing) certain data in the first place.

---

[1]   J. H. Saltzer and M. D. Schroeder, "The Protection of Information in Computer Systems," *Proceedings of the IEEE*, Vol. 63, No. 9, September 1975, pp. 1278–1308; see also http://en.wikipedia.org/wiki/Principle_of_least_privilege.

Ring 2: Neutralize Attacks

The challenge of deflecting and defeating attacks is both central to the task of minimizing the expected costs of cyberattack and the source of the greatest number and diversity of more specific actions (more accurately, classes of actions) entailed in a more general action. Accordingly, the Cyber Sunburst Graph identifies the following actions as collectively encompassing the variegated efforts needed to protect systems from attack:

- Reduce the number of cyberattack attempts.
- Develop mitigations for specific known threats.
- Block cyberattacks.
- Ensure the quality of software and hardware components in the network.
- Systematically reduce risks inherent in the network.
- Improve the security-related competence of system administration.
- Test system defenses against simulated attacks.
- Reduce the amount of material exfiltrated in attacks.
- Increase distributed denial of service (DDOS) defenses.
- Counter the insider threat.

This portion of the Cyber Sunburst Graph is shown in Figure 3.2.

Many of the actions listed above (largely the first eight) are related to operational hygiene in that they involve preventative best practices that minimize an attacker's ability to exploit a computing system. A poorly managed system for which these measures have not been taken becomes easy prey. In contrast, DDOS and insider threat defenses are necessary regardless of an organization's computational best practices. The reader should also be reminded that these actions are *attempts* at neutralizing attacks; there are no guarantees that these actions will be successful.

Reduce the number of cyberattack attempts: This action addresses the environment in which hackers operate and extends beyond the confines of a single organization. Reducing the incentive for hacking and availability of hackers is only rarely a CISO responsibility, since it entails public policies associated with prosecution and deterrence. CISOs might contribute by conveying to hackers that going after their organization entails a great deal of frustration (deterrence by denial) or risk (e.g., via hack-backs).

Develop mitigations for specific known threats: This action comprises all elements of defense that start with information on specific threats. These mitigations then support various elements of defense, such as sandboxing bad packets (e.g., by developing new signatures for an intrusion detection/prevention system) or countering attacks in progress (e.g., by detecting network behaviors characteristic of attacks coming from particular threats).[2]

Block cyberattacks: This action tries to prevent an attack from gaining hold on a network. These defenses may take place at an organization's borders (e.g., at the firewall) or at the client device. Such defenses include automatic detection/eradication and user-aided defenses (e.g., not clicking on suspect links).

---

[2]   In a cybersecurity context, to *sandbox* a piece of code is to execute it in a restricted operating environment, where the resources that it can interact with are limited, and therefore the harm it can cause can be contained. For more information, see https://en.wikipedia.org/wiki/Sandbox_(computer_security).

Figure 3.2
The "Neutralize Attacks" Strategy with Actions

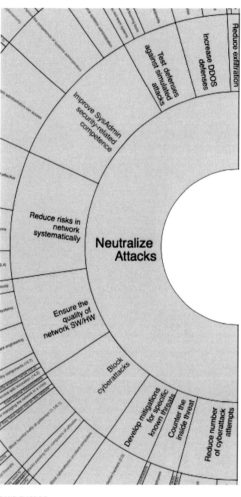

RAND *TL186-3.2*

Ensure the quality of software and hardware components in the network: Systems are hacked because they have vulnerabilities (although a vulnerability-free system may be encounter risks from protocol weaknesses). Eradicating or at least reducing the number and criticality of these vulnerabilities makes systems harder to compromise.

Systematically reduce risks inherent in the network: Although this action might come under "Ensure the quality of software and hardware components in the network," it entails a broader examination of all weaknesses, including those that might creep in after they have (or appear to have) been eradicated. This action is focused on system management more than system improvement.

Improve the security-related competence of system administration: Better system administration means better defense and requires better system administrators. This action was listed separately because improving the quality of personnel feeds not only most of the actions under stopping attacks but also certain actions under "manage exposure," "improve resilience," and "accelerate recovery."

Test system defenses against simulated attacks: Figuring out how far a competent attacker can get is an important step for serious organizations. The results from such an exercise inform other actions that can mitigate attacks (or find the right level of exposure).

Reduce the amount of material exfiltrated in attacks: This action comes into play if the attackers succeed in wresting control over information they are looking for. It can include blocking material, as well as anything that makes the attacker doubt the value of the material taken.

Increase DDOS defenses: A DDOS attack involves preventing legitimate use of a computing service by either disrupting or flooding the service. DDOS attacks are unique in that they can affect otherwise well-managed networks. The various defenses available include increasing the ratio of capacity to inflow and mitigating the ratio of processing/storage consumed to inflow levels.

Counter the insider threat: Although the percentage of mischief in cyberspace perpetrated from the outside (rather than the inside) is higher than it was 20 years ago (thanks to networking), the insider threat is still important, particularly for organizations that have taken pains to insulate themselves from the outside world (e.g., the National Security Agency [NSA]).

Ring 2: Increase Resilience

Increasing resilience involves preparing an organization so that is minimally affected if a cyber-attack is successful. It is supported by the following more specific actions:

- Take (specific) resilience steps.
- Conform to resilience guidelines.
- Improve cross-system engineering.

This portion of the Cyber Sunburst Graph is shown in Figure 3.3.

Figure 3.3
The "Increase Resilience" Strategy with Actions

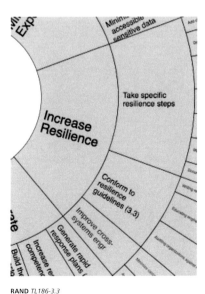

RAND *TL186-3.3*

Take resilience steps: This combines a number of specific steps (enumerated in the next ring). This particular general action is an example of a container made up of specific actions—rather than something that cannot take place or cannot take place as effectively until specific actions occur.

Conform to resilience guidelines: This action presumes the existence of guidelines that have been developed to inform and guide resilience actions. This action speaks to the importance of determining that the actions taken by the organization are consistent with and adequate for meeting such guidelines.

Improve cross-system engineering: An important element of resilience is managing cross-system dependency, minimizing the likelihood that faults in one subsystem can propagate through other subsystems, and reducing single-point failures (as well as common-mode failures).

Ring 2: Accelerate Recovery

Although the speed of a recovery from a cyberattack can only be known after the attack takes place and crucially depends on exertions made in the recovery phase, experience (notably with other sources of system failure) suggests that many actions taken prior to an attack can hasten the speed and lower the costs of a recovery. Accordingly, the general action of accelerating recovery can be facilitated if organizations take the following specific actions:

- Generate rapid response plans.
- Increase response competence.
- Build the ability to restore systems.
- Install systems to detect attacks quickly.
- Develop methods to rapidly isolate infected systems.
- Clean out malware from the system.

This portion of the Cyber Sunburst Graph is shown in Figure 3.4.

Figure 3.4
The "Accelerate Recovery" Strategy with Actions

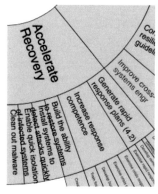

Generate rapid response plans: To respond, it helps to have a plan; to respond quickly, it helps to have a plan that mobilizes activity expeditiously. This action reflects an expectation that a rapid response plan can be written down, promulgated, and assessed by outsiders.

Increase response competence: This is the personnel management part of response. It entails having competent people with a combination of the required decision authority and sufficient knowledge and training.

Build the ability to restore systems: The ability to recover a system is a function, in part, of the ability to restore a system to its previous configuration (plus whatever features are necessary to forestall a repeat disaster). Just as systems can be built so that repair is, alternatively, easier or harder (e.g., are the spark plugs accessible?), systems can be built for faster or slower restoration.

Install systems to detect attacks quickly: This recovery method is specific to cyberattacks (as opposed to, for example, natural disasters). The sooner the attack can be detected (under the assumption that it proceeds deliberately, or at least diffuses at probabilistic rates), the faster it can be stopped, with correspondingly less damage to the availability of systems or to systems themselves. Note that this is a particular case of a specific capability that could *also* support a ring-zero objective of reducing the frequency and consequences of cyberattack.

Develop methods to rapidly isolate infected systems: This specific capability assumes that the attack in question has been detected. Given the detection and sufficient characterization of attacks that proceed non-instantaneously, methods that allow decoupling permit fault isolation, which in turn limits the damaged baseline from which recovery proceeds.

Clean out malware from the system: A critical aspect of the recovery phase (again, specific to cyberattack) is to ensure that whatever took down the systems is not present in the network to repeat the performance. The clean-out phase can sometimes last longer than the time required to recover functionality systematically, but it often entails reduced performance in the interim because network connections are limited to ensure against re-infection during cleanup.

CHAPTER FOUR

Ring 3

When considering the four actions of ring 1 (accelerate recovery, increase resilience, minimize exposure, and neutralize attacks), neutralizing attacks is uniquely associated with cybersecurity; resilience, recovery, and (to a slightly lesser degree) exposure minimization are all actions that may be taken for reasons other than cybersecurity, such as in preparation for a power outage or natural disaster.[1] Our work has been motivated by cybersecurity (as opposed to system management), and hence we have more detail on specific actions to block attacks. Furthermore, many specific actions under exposure control, recovery, and resilience are functions of the particulars of the system being defended and are therefore not displayed. By contrast, actions specific to cybersecurity can be generalized across systems (in part because of much software is standardized).

Accordingly, as one moves out from the center of the Cyber Sunburst Graph, more of the actions encountered will be descendants of the neutralizing attacks action. In addition, because of the tangible and imperative nature of neutralizing attacks, the corresponding parent-child relationships are dominated by action-prerequisite links (a general action requires specific actions) as opposed to composition (a general action is made up of many specific actions). For these reasons, we present the actions of ring 3 via a depth-first search order as opposed to the breadth-first search approach used for ring 2.[2]

Ring 3: Resilience → Take Resilience Steps

The subsidiary actions under "take resilience steps" are listed below:

- *Resilience → Take resilience steps → **Add channels:*** Redundant communication channels permit organizations to function (albeit sometimes at reduced levels of service) if primary communication channels suffer cyberattacks. Note that redundancy can be multifaceted. Many lines going into one router or running through common physical conduits offer little redundancy against upstream attacks.

- *Resilience → Take resilience steps → **Develop procedures to prioritize communications:*** U.S. military organizations have developed MINIMIZE (formal name) procedures to ensure that if channels are constrained, critical messages get priority over noncritical mes-

---

[1] Partnership for Disaster Resilience, *Post-Disaster Recovery Planning Forum: How-To Guide*, 2007.

[2] "Depth First vs. Breadth First," Github.com, 2012.

sages. Organizations that lack sufficiently redundant channels might well do something similar.

- *Resilience → Take resilience steps →* **Create backup power sources:** Electric power underlies everything electronic, and most IT power is provided for by continuous power sources (note that even in the case of battery-powered systems, there is an indirect dependence on continuous power sources in order to recharge the batteries). Thus, although the threat to an organization's power supply rarely materializes, few unprepared organizations can function if it does. Under this action are two specific actions:
  - Install backup power sources.
  - Practice using back-up power sources.

The importance of testing the operation and use of backup power sources cannot be overemphasized. One of the most powerful messages in *Normal Accidents*[3] was how often the assumption that the existence of backup limited the odds of disaster was vitiated by the failure of backup capabilities that, presumably, were never operated because they were, in fact, backup.

- *Resilience → Take resilience steps →* **Create duplicate assets where necessary:** This action is a more general version of the above action. It may refer to physical conduits, office equipment, machinery, etc.

- *Resilience → Take resilience steps →* **Develop and use un-erasable backups:** Backing up data is one of the most elementary steps that organizations can take to preserve business continuity in the face of disaster. Many organizations devote substantial resources to ensuring that at, any given point, the backups they have provide a precise duplicate of the primary files they are using. The emphasis on un-erasable is protection against a potential cyberattack that aims to erase (or alter) past records. In practice, this raises the question of how to protect or at least minimize the electronic buffer where information is stored prior to its archiving.

- *Resilience → Take resilience steps →* **Make it easy to sever misperforming subsystems:** The danger is that attacked subsystems can start sending other subsystems bytes, the quantity or quality of which put these other subsystems at risk. The ability to sever these communications (or just pull such subsystems offline) can provide some insulation against cascading failure.

- *Resilience → Take resilience steps →* **Document resilience steps:** Such documentation helps with assessment, explanation (if the rationale for a step is understood, these steps can be modified if underlying conditions), training, and establishing a baseline for managing new or changed hardware and software.

Ring 3: Resilience → Conform to Resilience Guidelines

- *Resilience → Conform to resilience guidelines →* **Write resilience standards** entails both developing the knowledge of what actions best (or most cost-effectively) promote resil-

---

[3]   Charles Perrow, *Normal Accidents: Living with High-Risk Technologies*, 2nd edition, New York: Basic Books, 1984.

ience, and coming to a sufficiently good consensus on what the knowledge indicates in terms of recommended practices. This action is called out in the DHS Blueprint as capability 3.3.

- *Resilience → Conform to resilience guidelines → **Educate engineers on resilience standards*** entails one or many of the following steps: adding resilience knowledge into engineering curricula, post-schooling inculcation of resilience knowledge (much of which is organization-specific), and ensuring that resilience is kept in mind when making engineering choices. Although organizations are responsible for the latter two, the former action is often carried out by external organizations (e.g., universities).

- *Resilience → Conform to resilience guidelines → **Audit against resilience standards:*** This action is called out in the DHS Blueprint as capability 3.5. It assumes such standards; a method for measuring conformance to such standards; a body of doctrine, practice, and norms for conducting audits; expectations for dealing with the results of such audits— and, of course, the audits themselves.

Ring 3: Resilience → Improve Cross-System Engineering

- *Resilience → Improve cross-system engineering → **Minimize cascading system failures:*** Engineering for the purpose of minimizing cascading failures is a tenet of system design, architecture, and management. In some cases, it may require analysis and reengineering of systems that were initially engineered without sufficient regard to risks (such as from cyberattacks). Under this action are several actions specific to single-points-of-failure (SPOFs)—functions whose failure portends the failure of the system overall:
  - ***Understand potential cascading effects*** with the potential to create SPOFs.
  - ***Eliminate SPOFs:*** This action limits the damage that can come when something is broken. This elimination, in turn, requires two actions:
    - ***Find SPOFs:*** The ability to understand a system well enough to find every feature in the system whose failure could imperil the entire system is simultaneously rewarding and difficult. The 2003 Northeast power outage intensified efforts to find SPOFs within the North American power grid, but the difficulty of doing so correctly was illustrated by a multistate (and international) power outage that struck the Southwest in 2009.[4] Understanding potential cascading effects with the potential to create SPOFs is DHS Blueprint capability 3.1.
    - ***Mitigate SPOFs:*** SPOF elimination is specific to the system. Redundancy is a common way to eliminate SPOFs (if there are adequate procedures for bringing spare capacity into play), but others are possible (e.g., having recipient operations default to more reasonable sets of actions if subsystems fail to deliver).

- *Resilience → Improve cross-system engineering → **Avoid common-mode failure in software:*** Redundancy may also extend to the software layer, so that attacks on one operating

---

[4] Federal Energy Regulatory Commission and North American Electric Reliability Corporation, *Arizona-Southern California Outages on September 8, 2011: Causes and Recommendations*, April 2012.

system, for instance, leave some routers and/or servers up even if most are down.[5] This is recommended only if the security benefits from multiple protocols are not overwhelmed by the additional insecurity associated with managing heterogeneous systems. Under this action come two specific actions:

- *Develop ways to create software diversity:* Organizations can deliberately diversify their software. Yet few, if any, organizations can, on their own, change the basic tendency within the IT world to converge on a single dominant software supplier. In that this action is DHS Blueprint capability 9.4, this may be a job for government (or national governments working together). Under this action is a more specific action:
  - *Seek alternative software architectures,* which entails actively searching out alternatives to mainstream products for particular applications. Often these alternatives are open-source products,[6] which have specific security advantages (they tend to be simpler which gives them a smaller attack surface, and are user-customizable for those who prefer greater security) and disadvantages (see Heartbleed).
- *Create standards that facilitate the smooth use of heterogeneous software:* The role of standards is to allow heterogeneous software applications to work together in ways that homogenous software applications can through the use of proprietary data standards, API (application programmer interface), and data communications protocols. The work of developing standards, as noted above, entails writing a good standard, getting it approved, and then persuading enough software developers to adopt it, even if only as an option alongside their proprietary protocols.

Ring 3: Recovery → Generate Rapid Response Plans

- *Recovery → Generate rapid response plans → Draft rapid response plans:* Drafting rapid response plans is an organizational responsibility (rather than something that can be usefully standardized or made mandatory). It relates specified contingencies to specified recovery actions, and, in large organizations, indicates who has what responsibility for action (rather than detailing which actions need to be performed when).

- *Recovery → Generate rapid response plans → Develop partnerships for rapid recovery:* Developing partnerships for rapid recovery is something that takes place among organizations. These partnerships can be vertical: Organizations can make emergency arrangements with their suppliers (and can offer alternatives for and manage expectations of their customers). They can also be horizontal, involving, for instance sharing arrangements or working together to allocate scarce resources and cover each other's customers in emergencies. This is DHS Blueprint capability 4.3.

- *Recovery → Generate rapid response plans → Develop remediation plans consistent with standards:* Each plan would be specific to the organization but would presumably be influenced by broadly understood best practices. This is DHS Blueprint capability 4.2.

---

[5] See, for instance, Daniel Geer, Rebecca Bace, Peter Gutmann, Perry Metzger, Charles P. Pfleeger, John S. Quarterman, and Bruce Schneier, "Cyber*In*security: The Cost of Monopoly," *Computer and Communications Industry Association Report,* September 2003.

[6] For example, Foxit as a substitute for Adobe's products.

- *Recovery → Generate rapid response plans → **Exercise rapid response plans:*** Organizations would develop exercises that would presume a cyberattack and its attendant effect on its systems, and then go through recommended recovery operations. These exercises can be tabletop or real-world. A specific action associated with exercising such plans would be to assess the rapid responses to determine the organization's readiness and make appropriate fixes. This is DHS Blueprint capability 5.4.

Ring 3: Recovery → Increase Response Competence

- *Recovery → Increase response competence → **Exercise crisis response within sectors:*** The value of this action (DHS Blueprint capability 5.2) presumes that a crisis response that is exercised within one organization would not be indicative of behavior in a real crisis, either because its assumptions are optimistic (access to resources considered ample may be limited if other organizations within the sector lay claim to them) or pessimistic (resources may be acquired from other organizations in a crisis). A crisis response exercise with external participants allows good ideas to spread among organizations.

- *Recovery → Increase response competence → **Exercise crisis response across sectors:*** This is DHS Blueprint capability 5.1. It can help if intersectoral exercises allow organizations to have a better idea of how they would response to crises than if the exercises were confined to the sector. Yet to be determined is what kind of plausible cyberattack scenario would have effects that cross organizations that do not share information systems, or, at worst, share access to common utilities (interference with which has significant downstream effects). More work is also needed to understand the distribution of effects from various cyberattacks and how they may resemble or differ from the distribution of effects from other calamities, whether deliberate, accidental, or natural.

- *Recovery → Increase response competence → **Develop business continuity plans:*** Developing business continuity plans is a specific element that mixes resilience (as hinted at by "continuity") and recovery (if minor interruptions in service are tolerable). These plans define core business functions, allowable deviations from such functions in emergencies, and plans to recover such functions using alternative capabilities. This is DHS Blueprint capability 5.3.

- *Recovery → Increase response competence → **Train first responders:*** An important element of recovery is keeping things from getting worse immediately. First responders are an important element in preventing excess loss from cyberattacks that lead to the denial of (physical) services (e.g., natural gas) or those that lead to destruction (e.g., a hacked chemical plant that starts a major fire).

Ring 3: Recovery → Build the Ability to Restore Systems

- *Recovery → Build the ability to restore systems → **Create a priority data plan:*** A priority data plan would identify which data (or data streams) are most critical for business continuity and take steps to ensure continued access to such data (streams) in a crisis.

Ring 3: Exposure → Reduce the Number of Networked Machines

Although four subsidiary actions were identified as comprising the minimization of unnecessary exposure, more specific actions were identified for only one of these four: reducing the number of networked machines. The children of this action are listed below:

- *Exposure → Reduce the number of networked machines → **Reduce the number of externally addressable machines:*** We distinguish between those machines that can be accessed because they are connected to a directly addressable machine (e.g., a printer hanging on a personal computer) and those that can be accessed because they are directly addressable (e.g., a network printer with an Internet Protocol [IP] address). Although indirectly accessible machines are still at risk (e.g., a computer can be compromised through cyberattack and thereby commanded to feed the printer harmful commands, leading perhaps to the printer's destruction), removing direct addressing reduces the number of ways the printer can be attacked (a.k.a. its attack surface).

- *Exposure → Reduce the number of networked machines → **Determine which systems should be isolated:*** This is an analytic function in which the risk to systems has to be traded off against the cost and inconvenience associated with not allowing networked machines or the outside world to access the systems. Further analysis would be required to determine trade-offs between virtual (e.g., cryptographic) isolation (to permit tunneling communications links over otherwise open networks) and physical isolation, as well as policies for intermittent access (e.g., via removable media) or radio-frequency access (thus requiring understanding of how large a physical perimeter needs to be guarded).

- *Exposure → Reduce the number of networked machines → **Isolate systems as per this determination:*** In many cases, this entails disconnecting systems that were previously connected (or encrypting links that were previously unencrypted, etc.).

- *Exposure → Reduce the number of networked machines → **Test isolation:*** Many organizations that believe their systems to be isolated are in error, either because they have not thoroughly understood what isolation entails, or because there are undocumented connections that make them accessible. Ensuring isolation requires testing and retesting potential access methods in order to determine that the degree of isolation is consistent with isolation policies. Shodan (www.shodanhq.com) is one such tool for doing so.
  - ***Tools for testing isolation:*** A prerequisite action is *acquiring and/or developing tools for testing isolation.* Organizations can decide to buy or not buy, but if the tool has to be developed, external vendors are usually the ones to do so; such developments can be encouraged by government R&D and/or acquisition policy.

Note that the above statement about development is true for the development of any capability and will not be explicitly repeated for the capabilities below.

Ring 3: Neutralize Attack → Reduce the Number of Cyberattack Attempts

As noted in the diagram, there are ten actions that come under the general action of neutralizing attacks. All of them have subsidiary actions. Reducing the number of hackers entails three subsidiary actions:

- *Neutralize Attack → Reduce the number of cyberattack attempts → **Reduce the number of hackers:*** This action assumes that the fewer people who could hack are in a position to hack, the lower the threat from hacking. Hackers could be put out of commission in one of two ways:
  - ***Finding employment for would-be hackers***, notably but not exclusively in cybersecurity, can meet both the income and psychological needs of many hackers, and may thereby reduce their illicit hacking. After the Cold War, for instance, the West endeavored to employ Soviet nuclear scientists to keep the latter out of mischief (notably away from potential nuclear states). The efficiency of alternative employment remains to be seen. Hackers, unlike nuclear scientists, can moonlight from home, and potential employers have to be careful that they are not putting themselves at risk by hiring them.
  - ***Prosecute cybercrimes:*** Restraints available through prosecution (DHS Blueprint capability 1.2) entail incarceration, alternative institutionalization, or sufficiently restrictive probation. Prosecution, in turn, has its own prerequisites. This action affects (and hence is a child of) both "reduce the number of hackers" and "reduce the incentive to hack."
    - ***Investigate cybercrimes:*** The investigation of cybercrimes (DHS Blueprint capability 4.4) is currently performed by the FBI, the U.S. Secret Service, and, in some cases, state and local officials. It entails the usual law enforcement methods and has several prerequisites:
      - » ***Finding capable investigators*** is largely a matter of finding and training the right people.
      - » ***Developing investigative tools*** is largely a matter of their being developed either by the government or by its suppliers (there is some private interest in forensics for the purpose of characterizing attacks and how they escaped an organization's defenses but the interest in attribution is less).
      - » ***Collecting computer forensics***, in turn, rests on *persuading system owners to allow the collection of evidence from their systems.* In the United States, persuasion is becoming easier because organizations are increasingly aware of what they have at risk from hacking (the FBI, if it has to, can subpoena evidence, but putting together a case when the target is uncooperative is more difficult, and the FBI, with its large unmet backlog of cybercrimes, has a choice over which it will prosecute). Overseas, however, cooperation is less likely, and in places such as Russia or China highly unlikely.
    - ***Apprehend hackers:*** The ability to apprehend hackers, once they are identified by name (rather than their online handle), is straightforward in the United States, but

much less clear in most countries[7] and, again, impossible in Russia or China (no one quoted in the press believes the five People's Liberation Army members indicted by the United States in May 2014 will appear in a U.S. court). Thus, a prerequisite is to *persuade other countries to allow their citizens to be brought to justice* for cybercrimes.

- *Neutralize Attack* → *Reduce the number of cyberattack attempts* → *Reduce the incentive to hack:* The action is meant to put a thumb on the go/no-go decision for the hacker by increasing the risks associated with hacking (decreasing the gain from hacking is usually a side effect of efforts made to reduce the costs to the organization that was or could be hacked). Five prerequisites are associated with this action:
  - *Prosecute cybercrimes*: Covered above.
  - *Instilling ethics in hackers* is presumably what the insertion of ethics classes, notably, in high schools (and college courses for computer majors) is supposed to do.
  - *Putting the systems of hackers at risk* is one of the motivations for "hack-backs" (although it can also be used in service of prosecution[8]). The notion of a hack-back is that if the hackers—or at least their machines—can be put at risk because of hacking, that some of them (notably the less serious ones) will recalculate the costs and benefits of hacking and thereby desist. A more plausible motive for the CISO to authorize such activity is to redirect the hackers' attention to other, less dangerous potential targets. No organization admits to hacking back, but rumors that organizations do this still circulate.
  - *Writing laws that facilitate hack-backs* to enable the general action of putting the system of hackers at risk.
  - *Take action against cyber/crimeware markets:* Cybercrime markets create channels through which hackers can buy tools and sell their take without having to acquire the requisite computer expertise.[9] This action recognizes the growth of these markets and channels and takes action against them.

- *Neutralize Attack* → *Reduce the number of cyberattack attempts* → *Preempt attacks upon discovery:* Preempting attacks upon spotting them assumes indications of an attack that are good enough to permit them to be disrupted. This is typically a government function because of its intelligence capabilities,[10] although some private organizations tout similar capabilities to do some of this.

---

[7]   Kim Zetter, "Pentagon Hacker McKinnon Wins 10-Year Extradition Battle," *Wired.com*, October 16, 2012.

[8]   Charlie Osborne, "Georgia Turns the Tables on Russian Hacker," *ZDNet.com*, October 30, 2012. The target planted malware in a file that the hacker took; the hacker's computer was infected when the file was open and the infection turned on the webcam thereby photographing the presumed hacker.

[9]   Lillian Ablon, Martin C. Libicki, and Andrea A. Golay, *Markets for Cybercrime Tools and Stolen Data: Hackers' Bazaar*, Santa Monica, Calif.: RAND Corporation, RR-610-JNI, 2014.

[10]   Ellen Nakashima, "Pentagon Cyber Unit Wants to 'Get Inside the Bad Guy's Head,'" *Washington Post*, June 19, 2014.

Ring 3: Neutralize Attack → Counter the Insider Threat

- *Neutralize Attack* → *Counter the insider threat* → ***Physically secure computing spaces:*** This action assumes that the hacker is on or near the machines themselves, or has built or corrupted devices on or near the machines.[11] Several pathways have to be blocked. Doing so entails preventing hackers from getting inside the physical perimeter, preventing rogue equipment from getting inside the radio-frequency perimeter,[12] and managing the supply chain so that rogue equipment is not substituted for uncorrupted equipment (supply chain management is discussed further below).

- *Neutralize Attack* → *Counter the insider threat* → ***Reduce attacks by employees:*** This action addresses authorized users acting in rogue ways (the actions of unwitting insiders is a different matter discussed further below), or at least assuming privileges on the system that they are not entitled to. Apart from actions previously covered under reducing unnecessary exposure (e.g., least-privilege) specific actions to facilitate the reduction of insider attacks entail:
  - ***Vet employees:*** Organizations would vet employees (a category which includes anyone with system privileges) to ensure that they do not include those inclined toward mischief, whether out of gain, fear (e.g., blackmail), or ideology. The security clearance process is supposed to do this for the government (the notion of requiring a security clearance for critical infrastructure workers comes up from time to time).
  - ***Inculcate employees with the values of the organization:*** The point of inculcating employees with the values of the organization is to remind them of why it is important that they not betray their organization by subverting the security of the networks they use (this inculcation may also be useful against unwitting employee subversion such as might happen from, say, going to a bad website).
  - ***Monitor employees:*** Organizations must monitor employees for many reasons to be assured that they are not engaging in cyberattacks. One purpose is to determine whether an employee's actions, which each seem innocent, are collectively inexplicable unless the employee is pursuing other purposes. For example, the FBI had a monitoring system that logged access requests to its central computer system that should have caught Robert Hanssen had the FBI been more diligent about analyzing the data the monitoring system was collecting.
  - ***Force vacations and/or rotations:*** This action allows someone else to examine records in the individual's temporary or permanent absence. This originated as common practice in the banking industry (against embezzlement), and its relevance persists.

- *Attack* → *Counter the insider threat* → ***Limit privileges of contractors:*** In addition to steps for avoiding employee actions, steps could be taken for contractors that work for an organization.

---

[11] David E. Sanger and Thom Shanker, "N.S.A. Devises Radio Pathway into Computers," *New York Times,* January 14, 2014.

[12] This is the distance from which a signal can be intercepted from or interjected into a network. Note that this perimeter is not fixed. A rogue device with a powerful transmitter and/or antenna can operate from farther away. This threat can be assuaged by using link-to-link encryption.

Ring 3: Neutralize Attack → Develop Mitigations for Specific Known Threats

- *Neutralize Attack → Develop mitigations for specific known threats →* **Develop ways to identify and characterize hackers:** The ability to identify particular hackers helps in pre-attack input filtering (e.g., by creating signatures that intrusion detection systems can use in blocking suspect inputs, such as email or web pages). It can also help identify traces of attacks after they happen. This is DHS Blueprint capability 2.3. The ability to characterize specific attackers depends on two abilities:
  - **Collecting intelligence on cyberspace threats** is straightforward. The NSA penetrates networks to understand what potential hackers might be doing and how they might be doing it.[13] However, such intelligence is also being collected by private companies; e.g., Crowdstrike, which claims to track 60 such groups.[14]
    - ○ **Development of a capability to rapidly correlate information from disparate sources** supports the goal of determining identities in cyberspace. This is DHS Blueprint capability 6.2—a form of data fusion that requires a high level of intelligent information-sharing that may, it is hoped, be assisted by automated methods.
      - » **Bring the Advanced Malware Analysis Center to full operational capability:** This center is operated by the U.S. Computer Emergency Readiness Team. The hope is that malware artifacts can be assessed in terms of both what they say about their developer and what they say about the systems they were designed to attack.
  - **Assess the risk from various threat actors:** This action entails evaluating various groups to determine which pose a greater threat than others, as well as differentiating the targets most likely to appeal to particular groups (e.g., some groups are interested in stealing intellectual property, while others carry out financial crimes).
  - **Techniques to trap the tracks of and thereby characterize threat actors** might include but are not limited to honeynets and honeypots. The goal is to challenge hackers to reveal something about themselves that differentiates them from others.
  - **Standard ways to characterize threats** refer to common nomenclatures and methodologies. A specific prerequisite action would be to establish a community of interest in characterizing these threats in a standard method—DHS Blueprint capability 1.5.

Ring 3: Neutralize Attack → Block Cyberattacks

This is the form of cyberdefense that is most redolent of defense overall: active measures taken at the time of attack to repulse the hacker's attempts to penetrate a system or repulse the hacker's ability to extend the reach of an attack. It is composed of several specific actions:

- *Neutralize Attack → Block cyberattacks →* **Block cyberattacks on client computers:** Blocking attacks on client computers (e.g., PCs) not only keeps them clean (infected computers can be bricked or recruited into a DDOS attack that might be directed against the organization as well as external targets), but denies hackers a common pathway into

---

[13] Preventing cyberattacks featured prominently in President Obama's defense of the NSA; "Transcript of President Obama's Jan. 17 Speech on NSA Reforms," *Washington Post*, January 17, 2014.

[14] See www.crowdstrike.com.

organizations. A hacker who has compromised a computer inside the perimeter can infect others more easily, since such computers often have privileged access to information not obtainable from the outside (corporate executives are often prime targets of phishing precisely because of their extensive privileges). The odds of such an attack can be reduced by taking either or both of the following actions:

- *Encourage citizen awareness of Internet risks:* This action helps ensure that current and future employees have some basic knowledge of cybersecurity and correct behavior on their machine. This is a function either of governments (at multiple level), nonprofit institutions, or profit-making institutions working in the public interest.

- *Train users in computer security:* This action is a common function—perhaps the most common—of CISOs; many wish the training were more frequent and more intense, not so much to bring users to a higher level of knowledge but to a higher level of awareness. This action has two components:

  ◦ *Development of education materials* is likely to be a vendor activity. Such materials would likely be characterized by a stronger engagement with students and longer retention time of lessons (both in terms of what is remembered and what students are aware of).

  ◦ *Development of testing materials* is also likely a vendor activity. Although testing materials are normally blended into education materials, some organizations have developed or acquired their own tests in order to find those with potential to be cybersecurity professionals within their own organization.

- *Neutralize Attack* → *Block cyberattacks* → *Develop best client practices:* DHS Blueprint capability 11.2 entails ensuring that users make sound choices whenever they are presented with choices by their software (or hardware, in some cases). Some of this is a matter of training, but correctness also results from software that makes it clear what users are choosing and in ways that are not at great variance with their expectations.[15]

  - *Develop usability requirements for human-computer interfaces*: An important prerequisite is to develop usability requirements for human-computer interfaces (DHS Blueprint capability 13.1), which is a matter of research into human factors, design knowledge, and incentives that favor the application of good human-computer interaction.

- *Neutralize Attack* → *Block cyberattacks* → *Vet employees likely to be unwitting conduits for attack:* Vetting employees likely to be cybersecurity risks would improve user cybersecurity practices (by not hiring those least likely to do the job well), but it is a practice that can only be recommended for the most sensitive positions for which no more automatic means (e.g., software run at the most secure level) can be used.

- *Neutralize Attack* → *Block cyberattacks* → *Authenticate users securely:* Authenticating users better ensures that those who claim privileges on a system are who they say they are. There are two basic routes to better authentication:

  - *Improve single-factor authentication techniques:* Because the first route into a client computer (or a client account on a corporate server) is to guess a user's password, the *requirement for a stronger password* is often the most straightforward path to com-

---

[15] See, for instance, Ka-Ping Yee, "User Interaction Design for Secure Systems," in *Proceedings of the 4th International Conference on Information and Communications Security*, R. Deng et al., eds., LNCS 2513, Springer, 2002, pp. 278–290.

puter security. That noted, the strongest password (that users can plausibly hope to remember) or even the strongest pass-phrase is less effective than multifactor authentication (MFA).[16]

- ***Adopt multifactor authentication:*** The adoption of MFA is pretty much an accomplished fact within the federal government, but it is largely the exception outside it. MFA—typically a token and a PIN—is difficult to break directly without subverting all components. Most of the failure modes of one factor are not failure modes of the other factors (as long as users submit these only to sessions they or someone they trust initiates). Several specific actions would strengthen the use of MFA:
  - ***Improve tokens:*** Possible improvement in tokens might feature more ease-of-use (e.g., those that register via proximity rather than manual entry), as well as higher security (a hack on RSA in 2011 appears to have compromised the security of Lockheed-Martin's systems[17]).
  - ***Improve biometrics:*** Possible improvement in biometrics would look for modalities and devices that can satisfy often-in-conflict desiderata, such as ease-of-use, discrimination (simultaneously fewer false positives and false negatives), persistence (over time), and resistance to spoofing. Fingerprints are the gold standard, but fingerprint sensors could stand improvement, and live-ness tests may be needed in certain applications.

- *Neutralize Attack* → *Block cyberattacks* → ***Block cyberattacks passing from computers of affiliates:*** The ability to block cyberattacks passing from computers of affiliates would have saved Target Corporation a great deal of grief inasmuch as the attack on its systems originated from a feckless HVAC supplier who was given access to systems that, themselves, ultimately had links to the server that supplied point-of-sale machines with software updates.[18] There are several approaches that can be employed; they range from **vetting the practices of affiliates**, to **sandboxing traffic to and from such affiliates**, to **rigorously paring down the privileges afforded to affiliates**.

- *Neutralize Attack* → *Block cyberattacks* → ***Block harmful traffic at gateways:*** Blocking harmful traffic at gateways is considered a very high-profile action, inasmuch as it represents DHS Blueprint capabilities 1.1 and 6.1.[19] The government's superior ability to block malware also appears to be the prime justification for a government role in protecting critical infrastructure by blocking or helping to block harmful traffic at the gateway to such infrastructure. Modern firewalls are loaded with signature information containing not only suspicious byte patterns (as might appear in malware) but also suspicious IP addresses and other suspicious modalities associated with the attempt to deliver malware. Behind this action are four subsidiary actions:

---

[16] Federal News Radio Custom Media, "White House Cyber Czar's Goal: 'Kill The Password Dead,'" FederalNewsRadio.com, June 18, 2014.

[17] Angela Moscaritolo, "RSA Confirms Lockheed Hack Linked to SecurID Breach," *SC Magazine,* June 7, 2011.

[18] Brian Krebs, "Email Attack on Vendor Set Up Breach at Target," KrebsOnSecurity.com blog, February 12, 2014.

[19] Some of this is a matter of multiple-chaining. Although the primary purpose of Einstein III, the instantiation of these capabilities, is intrusion detection and prevention, an important secondary purpose is to collect information on attacks and share this information beyond the federal government.

- *Develop good firewalls:* The development of good firewalls entails multiple improvements to improve their speed and discrimination (blocking bad traffic without blocking too much good traffic) while managing direct costs (e.g., system acquisition and maintenance) and indirect costs (e.g., manpower to chase down alarms). Successful use has several additional attributes:
  - *Harvesting data from firewall logs* should continuously maintain and improve the fidelity of the firewall by ensuring that the signatures stay current. This information can be shared with others, or traded for comparable signatures.
  - *Establishing a watch data center, such as the National Cybersecurity and Communications Integration Center,* is an important component in any intrusion detection system/intrusion prevention system (IDS/IPS) insofar as it provides human oversight, an ability to do deeper forensics on malware detected in the firewall, and a defense against attacks from botnets (a heavyweight DDOS attack) that cannot be simply handled by dropping (or "black-holing") bad traffic.[20] This is DHS Blueprint capability 4.1.
  - The ability to *sandbox suspect incoming traffic* helps protect the network, inform users why their incoming traffic (e.g., suspect email attachments, malware-laded web results) will not be coming, and provide samples for later analysis.
- *Administer firewalls correctly:* Good IDS/IPS systems need adroit administration. One of the primary faults of traditional firewalls is that they can fail if the policy for how to administer them is a poor guide for what should or should not be let through, or if good policy is not well implemented in code and/or instructions.[21]
- *Block traffic from certain sites:* This is part and parcel of firewall management. Among other techniques, it uses the list of suspect IP addresses to ensure that no incoming traffic from these addresses reaches machines within the organization.
- *Put as many systems behind firewalls as possible:* This action appears elementary, but if one starts with disparate sets of systems that emerged organically, then getting their traffic rerouted through a limited number of access points is not trivial (it also requires that firewalls be built with enough capacity to handle line input with the inevitable growth of network traffic). This action has two prerequisites:
  - *Improve configuration management:* The point of improving configuration management is to be able to determine whether or not a particular machine is within the confines of the IDS/IPS system, although it has other purposes, as noted above (e.g., to determine whether systems are fully patched).
  - *Invest in host software:* Investing in host-based software is also necessary for configuration management to work. The host software[22] sits on the managed devices and talks to the various pieces of network, notably configuration, management software.

---

[20] To *black-hole* traffic on a network is to silently discard, or drop, it without informing the source that the data did not reach the recipient. For more information, see https://en.wikipedia.org/wiki/Black_hole_(networking).

[21] "It can take up to two months of full-time training for a security professional to learn to operate a modern, complex firewall. Even tiny configuration errors can expose protected equipment to an attack." Andrew Ginter, "13 Ways Your Firewall Could Fail You," Wired.com Innovation Insights blog, August 12, 2013.

[22] An example is the U.S. Department of Defense's Host Based Support Software (HBSS). See Defense Information Systems Agency, "HBSS," undated.

- *Neutralize Attack* → *Block cyberattacks* → **Find and block infections after they have taken root on the network:** Finding and blocking infections after they have taken root on the network is a second line of defense to be employed if malware is not blocked at an organization's perimeters. There are many techniques for doing so, including looking for indications of unusual activity on the network or scanning internally for traffic (e.g., packets, sessions) traveling among machines that has been deemed characteristic of an attack, or characteristic of a particular attack group. This action has a prerequisite of **installing systems to detect anomalies**, with the concomitant prerequisite of ensuring that those operating such systems can do so skillfully.

- *Neutralize Attack* → *Block cyberattacks* → **Improve procedures for managing the network in a crisis:** Improving procedures for managing networks in a crisis assumes that the administration of a network should be sensitive to the varying likelihood of its being under attack. To wit, as the threat increases, privileges are withdrawn and scrutiny increases; as it wanes, the opposite takes place (although, in practice, official practice is that security ratchets up while conformance to security strictures lags as the threat appears to recede). Of note are two prerequisites:
  - **Developing security practices tiered to various crisis levels** assumes tiered threat levels. The U.S. Department of Defense, for instance, has established INFOCONs (information operation conditions) keyed to the threat environment that it believes its networks are operating in; such conditions are keyed by a combination of external events (e.g., world crises) and threat indicators specific to cyberattack. Whatever, the source, a tiered series of conditions reasonably dictates a correspondingly tiered set of operational procedures.
  - **Identifying the country's minimum essential information infrastructure** is an action that would have to be undertaken by the government. It would assert that certain elements of the infrastructure need to be rigorously protected against cyberattacks. To have serious meaning, there would have to be (as-yet-nonexistent) policies keyed to the level of criticality of various systems.

- *Neutralize Attack* → *Block cyberattacks* → **Erect internal firewalls and/or filters:** The larger an organization, the more likely it is to have rogue employees, and the much tighter its security has to be on every outward-facing device to ensure that none are compromised. A sufficiently large organization is therefore very likely to be compromised—unless it has erected barriers to keep mischief at bay within a subsegment. These firewalls and filters also allow sensitive processes to be on the network with less sensitive ones, and permit isolating a fault so as to limit the damage it can do to an organization.

Ring 3: Neutralize Attack → Ensure the Quality of a System's Hardware and Software

- *Neutralize Attack* → *Ensure the quality of a system's hardware and software* → **Develop processes and designs that can co-evolve with innovation:** This action corresponds to DHS Blueprint capability 14.3. Products of sound design and process are those that will not become obsolete or insecure as technologies improve or as products come to market that change the nature of network flows. One example of a system that benefits from such processes and designs is National Strategy for Trusted Identity in Cyberspace (NSTIC) governance of the design of identity management systems.

- *Neutralize Attack → Ensure the quality of a system's hardware and software → **Adopt security-enabled hardware and software:*** The adoption of security-enabled hardware and software is DHS Blueprint capability 12.2. This is largely a matter of choosing hardware and software that has high levels of security, either as a default or as an option.

- *Neutralize Attack → Ensure the quality of a system's hardware and software → **Develop acquisition processes to ensure delivery of trustworthy components:*** The development of acquisition processes to ensure delivery of trustworthy components entails an ability to frustrate potential supply-chain attacks, whether by deliberate insertion of rogue elements or by a failure of component designers to pay sufficient attention to security so that vulnerabilities in their code and protocols are readily found by hackers.[23] Under this more general action are more specific ones:

    - ***Developing procedures to trace components in the supply chain*** is a matter of generating and adopting best practices for supply-chain risk management. The latter combines vetting suppliers (and passing such requirements down as far as necessary) and chain-of-custody procedures to prevent rogue components from being substituted for trusted ones.

    - ***Developing regulations to manage the risk from insecure components*** creates best-practice guidelines for government agencies and those regulated by the government (at this point, largely defense contractors whose behavior is a function of the contracts they sign). This is clearly a government, not a CISO, action.

    - ***Avoiding the use of risky components*** is a matter of will (risky components may cost less or perform better) and information (on what components are risky). Under this general action is an important prerequisite that there be a source of reliable information on which components are, in fact, risky. To wit, ***findings of corrupted products would have to be broadcast***. Products from Huawei have been called out (by the House Intelligence Committee[24]), but without evidence of a smoking gun, at least within its unclassified report. Similarly, official testimony that identified tampering did not say who did it.[25]

- *Neutralize Attack → Ensure the quality of a system's hardware and software → **Improve the knowledge behind the engineering of software and hardware*** calls for general improvements in people and tools behind the construction of logic-processing components, machines, and systems. The people side is based on education, training, up-to-date information, and best practices. Tools should facilitate building security into these products from design forward. Several specific actions are components of this broader action:

---

[23] Although some types of supply-chain flaws are clearly deliberate (e.g., if a special code is entered, the system exhibits unexpected behavior). But many flaws—such as a product straight from the factory that is already infected by malware—could be either. See, for instance, Gregg Keizer, "Best Buy Sold Infected Digital Picture Frames," *Computerworld.com*, January 23, 2008.

[24] Mike Rogers and C.A. Dutch Ruppersberger, *Investigative Report on the U.S. National Security Issues Posed by Chinese Telecommunications Companies Huawei and ZTE*, Washington, D.C.: U.S. House of Representatives, October 8, 2012.

[25] Josh Smith, "Homeland Security Official: Some Foreign-Made Electronics Compromise Cybersecurity," *NationalJournal.com*, July 7, 2011.

- *Improving the knowledge of essentials* entails the inculcation of security knowledge and security responsibilities for system designers. It should teach these designers to think like a hacker and be constantly mindful that the features inserted into systems to make them more flexible or user-friendly (e.g., the so-called security hint) also makes life easier for hackers (e.g., many of the answers that individuals offer are public knowledge). This action is DHS Blueprint capability 8.1.
  ◦ *Development of a common body of knowledge* is understood to be an academic endeavor that devolves into a common set of materials (e.g., books, or as a set of commonly understood principles). A knowledge base on which cybersecurity measures work cost-effectively and which do not work so well can be put to immediate use by CISOs in protecting their networks. This is DHS Blueprint capability 8.2.
- *Develop best practices for incorporating security into software development* is cousin to the development of knowledge of security practices in software development. This action is DHS Blueprint capability 12.3 and includes not just coding but also design, personnel management, testing, and inspection. Under this action is the helpful prerequisite of *using and enhancing specific best practices*, notably those *developed by MITRE/SANS on good coding.*[26]
- *Encourage the use of good coding techniques.*
- *Encourage intelligent practice for system architecture:* Encouraging intelligent practice for system architecture recognizes that secure software depends on design criteria as well as the quality of coding to ensure that the code matches design criteria. Examples include a comparison of Chrome versus Firefox (circa 2013) that concluded that although the number of vulnerabilities in both code bases was comparable in terms of total quantity, the former had ten times fewer critical vulnerabilities because of its privilege separation[27] (so that faults in the browser session did not propagate to the rest of the computer's software base). Similarly, consider Apple versus Android (circa 2012), in which the former had many more vulnerabilities but far less malware because of its closed ecology.[28]

• Neutralize Attack → *Ensure the quality of a system's hardware and software* → *Mitigate vulnerabilities in software:* Mitigating vulnerabilities in software refers to the process of identifying and eradicating faults in software that has already been brought to the market, and, in many cases, already installed. Systems are penetrated only because they have vulnerabilities. Some vulnerabilities are unknown to the software manufacturer (zero-day vulnerabilities) or have not been known long enough for a fix to have been developed. For others, patches have not been installed. Although the hardest targets require a zero-day exploit, most targets do not. This action has several prerequisites:
  - *Fixing software vulnerabilities quickly and thoroughly* does more for security than putting them off or scheduling them periodically but infrequently. This action is a combination of the following:

---

[26] Steve Christey, ed., *2011 CWE/SANS Top 25 Most Dangerous Software Errors*, The MITRE Corporation, September 13, 2011; see also The MITRE Corporation, "Common Weakness Enumeration," 2014.

[27] Matthew Finifter, Devdatta Akhawe, and David Wagner, "An Empirical Study of Vulnerability Rewards Programs," presented at USENIX Security, August 15, 2013.

[28] Symantec Corporation, *Internet Security Threat Report 2013*, Volume 18, Mountain View, Calif., 2013.

- *Finding software vulnerabilities quickly and thoroughly* is a matter of diligence on the part of software manufacturers prodded or at helped by outside entities. Progress at finding bugs can be helped by:

  » *Encouraging software makers to invest more resources in postmarket bug detection* may be a matter of cajoling, naming-and-shaming, or examining liability regimes that make software manufacturers responsible for the damage caused by the bugs in their products. However, leaning on software manufacturers has downsides (liability regimes are largely incompatible with open-source software, for instance).

  » *Developing tools that can find vulnerabilities* entails improving the efficiency by which defects in software can be found. Fuzzers, for instance, are tools that look for vulnerabilities by feeding software invalid, unexpected, or random data and seeing whether such data cause system crashes or other faults. Such tools are double-edged swords in the sense that their development may also allow bad hackers (black hats) to find faults before good hackers (white hats) do.

  » *Bug bounties* have proven efficient at garnering third-party participation in finding software faults. Bug bounty contributors now include Google, Microsoft, and Facebook. There are also third-party efforts, such as Pwn-to-Own and Pwnium. Currently, the total payoff for discovering bugs is in the single-digit millions of dollars (compared with the $70 billion being spent worldwide on cybersecurity every year). A dark side to the bug bounty business is that intelligence agencies worldwide are also interested in buying bugs for exploitation rather than mitigation. *Suppressing the government-funded gray market in vulnerabilities* may help boost the efficiency of bug bounty programs.

- *Creating software patches expeditiously* is up to software vendors. The measure of *expeditiously* normally depends on the severity of the fault: e.g., how easy it is to convert it into an exploit, what privileges hackers can acquire by exploiting the fault, and whether the configuration that permits the exploit is common and/or easily induced or rare and/or hard to induce.[29] Serious vulnerabilities might be patched within days or weeks (as Heartbleed was); patch times for the more subtle flaws discovered via Tipping Point's Zero-Day Initiative (zerodayinitiative.com) can take months. Oracle's initial refusal to patch a serious Java vulnerability until its quarterly patch cycle (Oracle later accelerated its patch) convinced many cybersecurity analysts to recommend that users uninstall their Java client.[30]

— *Deploying tools that can fix vulnerabilities* would facilitate automatic patch management. Such a tool would have to be quite sophisticated to deal with software that might be broken by the patch (software becomes brittle that way when it circumvents those functions that govern access to the operating system, browser, or key attributes in the software it sits on and codes directly to lower-level functions). Prerequisites to the deployment of tools are as follows:

---

[29] A rogue charger can compromise an iPhone, but success at mounting such an attack requires onsite presence and a careless user (Timothy Lord, "iPhone Hacked In Under 60 Seconds Using Malicious Charger," Slashdot.com blog, August 2, 2013).

[30] Brian Krebs, "Security Fix for Critical Java Flaw Released," KrebsOnSecurity.com blog, August 30, 2012.

- ◦ The ***development of tools*** is likely to be taken up either by the vendor or open-source community.
  - ◦ The ***development of know-how*** is likely to be an internal organizational function. This action, DHS Blueprint capability 2.6, is a broader category of capability than its placement under the general action (deploying tools to fix vulnerabilities) indicates but was located here for tractability.
  - – ***Developing ways to tell users that their devices/systems are or may be infected*** is DHS Blueprint capability 11.3. Such tools would not only permit users to understand how vulnerable their machines are, but, in that many users are indifferent to security, similar tools could usefully inform system administrators which computers need to be upgraded. Upgrading can be understood as patch installation (see below), but also warnings about machines whose security settings are inappropriate or contrary to policy. For critical physical infrastructure (e.g., Supervisory Control And Data Acquisition [SCADA] systems and other machine controls), the issue may be ascertaining the existence and status of Internet-facing nodes.
  - – ***Employing tools that can find system vulnerabilities*** (as opposed to software vulnerabilities) would also help keep systems secure. These tools could be part of a broader systems configuration suite.
- Neutralize Attack → *Ensure the quality of a system's hardware and software* → ***Patch systems expeditiously:*** Patching systems expeditiously is necessary if the vendor-provided patches are going to do any good. It has two helpful prerequisites:
  - – ***Figuring out what patches needs to be installed*** entails organizations finding out when their software needs to be patched. This action, in turn, depends on the development of some sort of *broadcasting capabilities* either from vendors directly or from intermediaries.
  - – ***Developing software to automatically manage patches*** is a matter of system management. For all but the largest and/or most sophisticated organizations, it is likely to come from software vendors rather than developed internally.

Ring 3: Neutralize Attack → Systematically Reduce Risks Inherent in the Network

This is a facet of system management that calls for constant review and revision of the network's various settings, protocols, software, and policies. It has three components:

- *Neutralize Attack → Systematically reduce risks inherent in the network →* ***Ensure performance standards for cyber risk management are met:*** Ensuring that performance standards for cyber risk management are met is a matter of determining whether the performance standards incumbent on system administrators—emerging from a voluntary consensus process led by the National Institute of Standards and Technology (NIST)—are discharged in a satisfactory manner. This would be a CISO (or higher-level) responsibility, and is DHS Blueprint capability 2.4.

- *Neutralize Attack → Systematically reduce risks inherent in the network →* ***Develop sets of mitigation actions:*** Developing sets of mitigation actions translates these performance standards into actions to be taken. This requires knowledge of the standards, the accurate and timely understanding of the network's shortfalls, the resources to fix the shortfalls, and the command-and-control required to get the shortfalls fixed and ensure that they are in fact fixed. Accordingly, two prerequisites can be identified:

— *Identify necessary actions:* The identification of necessary actions would convert real-time reports on network activity to indications of where such activity may be indications of vulnerabilities (or worse, hostile activity) and thence to a plan of actions and milestones that address shortfalls expeditiously and cost-effectively. This function, in turn, entails *the use of network management tools*, themselves, a specific action that has two prerequisites:

  ○ *Develop a superior suite of network management tools:* The development of a superior suite of network management tools is largely a vendor responsibility coupled with the input of users, acting as advisors and potential buyers. This is DHS Blueprint capability 2.5.

  ○ *Develop guidelines for the use of network management tools:* The development of guidelines for the use of network management tools is closer to a set of best-practice guidelines. This responsibility could be taken up by the vendors, themselves, although more general guidelines could be generated by government and/or professional groups. This is DHS Blueprint capability 2.2.

— *Operate blue teams to ensure that actions are carried out:* Blue teams ensure that mitigation actions are carried out at the system, subsystem, and machine levels. Over time, technology should allow the automation of much of what they do—with the caveat that systems unconnected to the main network's management systems may require hand management longer.

- *Neutralize Attack → Systematically reduce risks inherent in the network → Incorporate new technology when cost-effective:* The incorporation of new technology when cost-effective is a way to ensure that organizations have the ability to secure themselves in the face of the constant contest between measure and countermeasure. New technologies would make it easier to, for instance, ensure that the network is up to date, detect hostile activity, and confound threat actions. This action has several prerequisites:

— *Encouraging innovation in new technologies (to address emerging threats)* incorporates the general suite of federal policies that facilitate technological development including direct funding, tax policies, intellectual property laws, market research, and creating federal buying pools. This is DHS Blueprint capability 12.6. Contributing to this goal could be the *development of public-private partnerships for commercial cybersecurity innovation.*

— *Focusing R&D on key security priorities* is a process by which the government systematically assesses the needs of cybersecurity to direct government dollars to where private dollars (motivated, not unexpectedly, by market signals) are not doing enough. This is DHS Blueprint capability 3.1. It has two prerequisites:

  ○ A *process to evaluate cybersecurity R&D* necessarily involves a multifaceted comparison that considers the goals of the R&D (cybersecurity's highest unmet needs) and the likelihood that the research approach can fulfill the goals that it sets out.

  ○ The *prioritization of R&D as per the Comprehensive National Cybersecurity Initiative* (CNCI; The White House, 2009) serves to drive federal cybersecurity

R&D in the directions indicated by the CNCI, as promulgated in 2008 and updated since then. This is DHS Blueprint capability 3.3.

- The ability to **evaluate security products** entails developing expertise, an organizational home, and the reputation to make comparisons among competing security products. As a rule, NIST avoids doing so directly, but it certifies laboratories that can do this. Whether or not sufficient and sufficiently good laboratories exist for cybersecurity are policy questions. This is DHS Blueprint capability 12.4. One subcomponent of this capability is the development of supply-chain risk management capabilities.
- **Transition R&D rapidly into use:** Policies to ensure that R&D advancements see network use quickly may include ways to disseminate and evaluate results faster, the encouragement of professional societies, and favorable tax and regulatory treatment of technology uptake (many of which have a broader applicability and cost-benefit considerations beyond cyberspace). This is DHS Blueprint capability 3.2.

Ring 3: Neutralize Attack → Improve the Security-Related Competence of System Administrators

To give this action the importance it deserves (and to maintain the strictly hierarchical nature of the Cyber Sunburst Graph), this action was treated as separate even though it is an input to almost all other actions. This action has several prerequisites:

- *Neutralize Attack → Improve the security-related competence of system administrators →* **Improve the information that system administrators can access:** The impetus for improving the information that system administrators can access speaks to the importance of both a common body of knowledge and the benefits of information-sharing. Although some information-sharing goes from machine to machine, much of this information has to be understood to be used and thus currently goes to people. Hence the importance of improving the information that system administrators (and, by extension, their systems) can access. This information is expected to be threat-specific and up to date. This action has several elements:
  - **Gather data on attacks from similar organizations:** Gathering data on attacks from similar organizations is a key element of information-sharing. The development of ISACs (Information Sharing and Analysis Centers) implies that similar industries face similar threats. This is partially true (certain sectors have their own threats, such as cybercriminals, and certain sectors have potentially vulnerable machinery in common); it is also partially misleading insofar as office automation systems are universally similar, and thus the ways in which they are vulnerable and can be exploited are also similar. It has two prerequisites:
    - **Improve the quality of information being shared:** One way to improve the quality of information being shared is to format it in a standard way (and use standard minimum data elements) so that details and important facets are shared accurately; with standard formatting, what is currently shared only among people at people-speed

can one day be shared among machines at machine-speed.[31] It has a prerequisite of ***developing incident reporting guidelines***, (DHS Blueprint capability 1.6) which can be carried out by the government or by professional societies.

○ ***Find ways to share more information:*** Finding ways to share more information is tantamount to encouraging people to share information more completely and quickly. This is DHS Blueprint capability 7.3. It has several prerequisites:

» ***Write information-sharing agreements:*** (DHS Blueprint capability 1.4) This would occur among like companies (e.g., two chemical firms), in which each promises to share information about cyberattacks with the other, implemented as a confidence-building measure. A prerequisite is to ***develop data-portability methods to protect the sources of information***. This is DHS Blueprint capability 7.4, which is meant to assuage the fears of contributors that the original source of the information they provide might be discovered and thus the information needs to be obscured by standard ways of conveying information without conveying authorship.

» ***Establish incentives for information-sharing:*** Having incentives for information-sharing (DHS Blueprint capability 7.5) ought also to spur information-sharing agreements by tilting the reveal-withhold choice to "reveal." A prerequisite for this action is to ***develop the appropriate regulations*** (or, if need be, legislation) that would provide such incentives.

» ***Generate robust processes for information dissemination:*** Having robust processes for information dissemination (DHS Blueprint capability 7.1) should also facilitate information-sharing by removing barriers between the decision to share and the actual sharing itself, as well as ensuring that the information shared with an organization goes to the right people within it.

» ***Develop standardized languages for information-sharing agreements:*** Having standardized languages for information-sharing agreements (DHS Blueprint capability 6.4) would make it easier to draft such agreements by eliminating delays over word choice and assuring signatories that similar agreements have been agreed to by others.

– ***Gather tips on attacks from all others:*** In addition to gathering information from their cousins, so to speak, organizations can also profit by *gathering tips from others* outside the circle. These tips can range from best practices to indications and warning of potential threat activity. This has two facets:

○ ***Improving the quality of tips*** (DHS Blueprint capability 11.1) is a matter of developing tools and techniques to reduce false positives and concentrate on those tips that are more likely and better-characterized indications of attack.

○ ***Increasing the quantity of tips*** entails finding ways to get individuals and organization to be more sensitive to what would be a tip, more willing to surface their tips,

---

[31] The U.S. Department of Homeland Security's *Quadrennial Homeland Security Report 2014* mentions "machine speed" four times in its discussion of the cybersecurity mission, suggesting a future regime in which indications and warnings can be passed among machines without necessarily being vetted or even seen by humans. Because such a capability is, at best, nascent, the cyber sunburst discusses information sharing in the context of improving what cybersecurity professionals know, while acknowledging that, in the future, shared information may be prerequisite to more than one action.

and more capable of rendering their information in ways and through channels that garner appropriate levels of attention. It requires ***increasing public awareness of the need for cybersecurity tips***, which one can think of as the cybersecurity equivalent of "if you see something, say something." This in turn would be facilitated by ***effective communications strategies for communicating risks*** (DHS Blueprint capability 7.3) as a way of using social media and other media to foster the increased production of risk and tip information.

– ***Generate information for stakeholders to permit automated responses:*** Generating information for stakeholders to permit automatic responses (DHS Blueprint capability 17.2) speaks to the potential transition from the provision of information to system administrators to the provision to automated systems (e.g., IDS/IPS). It has two prerequisites:

  ○ ***Establish a capability for automatic data exchange:*** This entails developing channels into which such information could be dropped that would be known to be reliable and which are in the right place, to be picked up by machines looking for such information. Reliability is not a given inasmuch as hackers may have considerable incentive to feed such a facilities false information—which, at very least, requires some spoof-resistant authentication methods. The development of public-private partnerships to foster automated data exchange might help.

  ○ ***Develop standard measures to share information on threat signatures:*** Developing standard methods to share information on threat signatures (DHS Blueprint capability 7.2) would make it easier to implement such agreements by making the exchange of information on threats easier, and, ultimately, in a form that can be sent to machines, not just individuals.

– ***Disseminate information on the efficacy of cybersecurity measures:*** The dissemination of efficiency information allows various stakeholders to evaluate alternative protocols, products, services, configurations, architectures, supply chains, and organizational processes in decreasing the spread and impact of hazards. It is DHS Blueprint capability 18.1.

• *Neutralize Attack* → *Improve the security-related competence of system administrators* → ***Improve the competence of system administrators:*** Improving the competence of system administrators would address the oft-stated difficulty of finding enough cybersecurity professionals and the less publicly stated difficulty of ensuring that those on the job have sufficient competence. Improving such competence has four components:

– ***Attract good people to cybersecurity:*** Attracting good people to cybersecurity helps maintain and improve the average competence of the cybersecurity workforce (in ways that attracting more people without regard to their quality does not). As a general rule, the attractions of any profession are a function of its emoluments, working conditions (including mission), and status—if these are high enough, people will be attracted. Over and above the basic laws of supply and demand, the following have been offered as ways to ease current supply/quality shortfalls:[32]

---

[32] See Martin C. Libicki, David Senty, and Julia Pollak, *Hackers Wanted: An Examination of the Cybersecurity Labor Market*, Santa Monica, Calif.: RAND Corporation, RR-430, 2014; especially Chapter Five.

- ◦ ***Recruiting foreigners*** entails not only reaching out to them, but changes in immigration law and policy that would let them stay in the United States. Enthusiasm for this measure should be tempered by understanding how much U.S. cybersecurity work is already done overseas,[33] coupled by the difficulty of using foreigners in national and domestic security positions.
- ◦ ***Using the Guard and Reserve for cybersecurity*** is also being touted as a solution to the cybersecurity problem within the national security community, but, again, caution is called for. Even if people doing similar work could be persuaded to join the Guard and Reserve (and assuming that their duties are focused on cybersecurity), the net improvement in managing cybersecurity in emergencies by shifting people to a military position (e.g., protecting a naval base) may be offset by their being shifted from a civilian position (e.g., protecting a bank).
- ◦ ***Generating incentives to induce people to be educated*** in cybersecurity is DHS Blueprint capability 10.2. One large scholarship-for-service program has attracted over 1,000 students to major in cybersecurity who then went to work for the federal government. Various other incentives may include those which raise the status of cybersecurity majors, allow them certain privileges, or guarantee first employment.
- ◦ A ***hackathon*** is a contest in which participants compete to defend systems against attack. These relatively inexpensive contests raise the profile of cybersecurity (the "cool" factor) and may thereby persuade people to consider cybersecurity as a profession.
- — ***Improve the education of cybersecurity professionals:*** Improving the education of cybersecurity professionals would help ensure that those with degrees have the skill sets required to secure systems. This general action could be furthered by two subsidiary actions:
  - ◦ ***Develop a rigorous cybersecurity curriculum*** is DHS Blueprint capability 10.1. The NSA has taken the lead, working with its counterparts in academia to develop a rigorous cybersecurity curriculum, notably those schools it has designated as Centers of Academic Excellence.
  - ◦ The ***certification of security professionals***, DHS Blueprint capability 10.4, refers to certifications such as CISSP (Certified Information Systems Security Professional), as well as those from specific corporations (e.g., Microsoft, Cisco). The belief is that such certifications are correlated with greater expertise at cybersecurity, although others such as the National Research Council argue that cybersecurity is an occupation, and is not yet ready to be a profession.[34]
- — ***Retain cybersecurity workers within the federal government:*** Retaining good cybersecurity people within the federal government, DHS Blueprint capability 10.3, is a challenge, particularly for those who can make more money in the private sector. As noted above, the quality of pay, working conditions, and status have a great deal to

---

[33] Target Corporation possessed (and ignored) the analysis from a malware detection tool made by FireEye Inc., that was operated by security specialists in Bangalore, India; Tiffany Kaiser, "Target Missed Early Warning Signs of Holiday Data Breach," *DailyTech.com*, March 13, 2014.

[34] National Research Council, *Professionalizing the Nation's Cybersecurity Workforce? Criteria for Decision-Making*, Washington, D.C.: National Academies Press, 2013.

do with job choice. It might help in achieving retention for the government to ***write workforce management regulations.***

- ***Improve system administrator capabilities:*** Improving the capabilities of existing system administrators is a matter of training, education, and, to some extent, selective weeding (although this is difficult to do with civil servants, many of those who administer federal networks are contractors). A component of this upgrading is ***adopting a skills maturity model***, DHS Blueprint capability 8.3.

- *Neutralize Attack* → *Improve the security-related competence of system administrators* → ***Outsource system administration:*** Outsourcing system administration is an option if the acquisition of competence cybersecurity professionals is difficult or cost-ineffective. It may also be considered as concomitant to other information management decisions, as illustrated by two forms of outsourcing:

  - ***Investigate cloud services:*** Cloud services may be adopted for any number of reasons, such as because they offer greater location-independence, or to harvest economies of scale in storage and processing. But outsourcing what are essentially servers to large companies that may specialize in offering cybersecurity (as part of their features package) may offer organizations the opportunity to improve cybersecurity in ways that may be more cost-effective than doing it themselves.[35]

  - ***Investigate security-as-a-service:*** Similarly, companies are investigating outsourcing for all or most their entire cybersecurity functions. Movement is slow, in part because this has traditionally been viewed as an organic duty, and partially because it means trusting a third party with access to one's data. Yet, there may be opportunities here to achieve similar or better security for less money.

Ring 3: Neutralize Attack → Test Systems Against Simulated Attacks

This is also known as red-teaming, of which pen(etration)-testing is an important component. Such tests can indicate in general how secure an organization's systems are and specific indicators of particular weaknesses to be fixed. This action has several components:

- *Neutralize Attack* → *Test systems against simulated attacks* → ***Deploy people to red-team systems:*** This entails hiring a team (either in house, or, more commonly, under contract). CISOs need a good sense of who the good red-teamers are, what they need to test, and under what ground rules. One way for DHS to acquire the services of such people is to ***leverage capabilities present at the NSA*** en route to perhaps being able to duplicate them on their own.

- *Neutralize Attack* → *Test systems against simulated attacks* → ***Acquire red-teaming tools:*** If the team is in-house, the organization will need to acquire red-teaming tools; contracted teams tend to bring their own such tools. However, the organization may also need tools to generalize from the results of the red team to find similar weaknesses throughout their systems.

---

[35] But with appropriate cautions: Dan Goodin, "AWS Console Breach Leads to Demise of Service with 'Proven' Backup Plan," *ArsTechnica.com*, June 18, 2014.

- *Neutralize Attack → Test systems against simulated attacks → **Use the results to prioritize subsequent investments:*** The last step, using results to prioritize subsequent investments, entails translating vulnerabilities found by what is invariably an elite set of hackers to vulnerabilities likely to be found by their potential attackers—and then prioritizing investments to reduce risks appropriately. This action suggests two adjunct actions:
  - ***Find evidence of failed attacks that suggest the possibility of future successful attacks:*** Although successful attacks normally cause a reassessment of an organization's security posture, attacks that failed because of failures at the last step also indicate weaknesses in an organization's security that allowed the attack to get as far as it did. Thus, evidence of failed attacks can suggest the possibility of future successful attacks.
  - ***Determine good investments as a result:*** Finally, CISOs can help determine good investments by examining the results of red-teaming and forensics on the system after failed attacks.

Ring 3: Neutralize Attack → Defend Against DDOS Attacks

DDOS attacks are a particularly difficult (although not yet extremely costly) problem in cyberspace because the faults that allow DDOS attacks are almost always in the systems of other people (e.g., individual bots) or institutions (e.g., the many Wordpress accounts hijacked to permit DDOS attacks on banks in late 2012[36]). There are two types of approaches that can be taken to reduce the impact of DDOS attacks:

- *Neutralize Attack → Defend against DDOS attacks → **Adopt counter-DDOS policies:*** Counter-DDOS policies are the providence of the federal government. They might include measures that could include, if deemed cost-effective, the following:
  - ***Holding Internet service providers responsible*** entails requiring them to detect infected computer users (presumably by looking at how many bytes they send out) and giving them the choice between cleaning their infections or losing Internet service. This would have to be a worldwide policy to do much good.
  - ***Minimizing unnecessary redirection services*** matters because many large DDOS attacks are carried out by sending small packets to redirection services, such as network time protocol, with the (falsified) return address of the target. The redirection service then sends large packets back to the target.[37]
  - The importance of ***providing DDOS mitigation to small sensitive sites*** arises because many victims of DDOS attacks are nongovernmental organizations who are taking on powerful but authoritarian or corrupt governments. Such mitigation can be achieved by hosting their sites on powerful networks.

---

[36]   Michael Mimoso, "Hackers Using Brute-Force Attacks to Harvest WordPress Sites," ThreatPost.com, April 15, 2013.

[37]   Lucian Constantin, "Attackers Use NTP Reflection in Huge DDoS Attack," *Computerworld.com,* February 11, 2014.

    – *Taking down botnets* can be done in many ways, such as hijacking their command-and-control servers. Microsoft worked with federal authorities to take down the Rustock botnet.[38]

- *Neutralize Attack → Defend against DDOS attacks → **Adopt counter-DDOS mitigations:*** Counter-DDOS mitigations are those that can be undertaken by organizations under threat of attack. They include the following:
  - *Acquiring more bandwidth:* DDOS attacks are meant to overwhelm the intakes of target organizations. One mitigation, adopted by many of the banking victims of the late 2012 DDOS attacks, is simply to acquire more bandwidth so as not to be overwhelmed by volume.
  - *Contract with anti-DDOS firms:* Another approach is to contract with anti-DDOS firms. Examples include hosting websites on capacious networks (e.g., Google's) or employing a content delivery service (whose original business was optimizing web content delivery through the adroit physical distribution of servers).
  - *Examine internal servers to prevent their crashing:* In some cases, DDOS attacks work not by overwhelming input pipes, but by overwhelming the ability of servers to process requests (e.g., an SQL [Structured Query Language] query). Examining such internal servers and either eradicating vulnerabilities that allow requests to eat up resources or black-holing illegitimate inputs could help.

Ring 3: Neutralize Attack → Reduce the Amount of Material Exfiltrated by Attacks

This can be divided into two components:

- *Neutralize Attack → Reduce the amount of material exfiltrated by attacks → **Reduce the quantity of exfiltrated data*** means that some or all data that hackers can acquire is prevented from leaving the organization. There are two ways to do this. The most common and reliable way is to ***establish a mail-guard*** of some sort that watches what leaves the network and blocks material that meets some criteria (e.g., going to an unknown address, containing proscribed words, exhibiting an unusual time/frequency pattern). There are several ways to defeat such a mail-guard, notably if hackers can pre-process the data (e.g., encrypt it or chop it up and ladle it into DNS [Domain Name System] calls), but such methods assume the data is acquired through remote code execution. Another way is to ***delete the data on an external intermediate system used by hackers*** (but this is legally problematic and will not work if the data has moved on or if hackers use redundant pathways).

- *Neutralize Attack → Reduce the amount of material exfiltrated by attacks → **Reduce the quality of exfiltrated data*** requires, essentially, poisoning the well by ***creating a honeypot from which hackers take false data***; ingesting false data would cast doubt on the

---

[38] Brian Krebs, "Rustock Botnet Flatlined, Spam Volumes Plummet," KrebsOnSecurity.com blog, March 16, 2011.

quality of the true data.[39] Although this method is trumpeted by proponents of active defense, there is little indication of how well it works. Some data is usable even in the face of contradictory data (e.g., one good password intermixed with nine bad passwords just means that hackers have to try something ten times), and other data is regarded as but a tile in a mosaic.

---

[39] "In response, more companies are resorting to countermeasures like planting false information on their own servers to mislead data thieves, patrolling online forums to watch for stolen information and creating 'honey pot' servers that gather information about intruders." Ian Urbina, "Hacker Tactic: Holding Data Hostage," *New York Times,* June 21, 2014.

CHAPTER FIVE

Using This Work

The organization of cyberdefensive actions presented in this report can be used in two fundamental ways: (1) to enable auditing of cyberdefensive resource allocation by a government or corporate organization that is evaluating the implementation of a cybersecurity strategy and (2) to serve as a prescriptive mechanism for consideration when an organization is developing a cybersecurity strategy. Both of these uses are intended for adoption by a wide variety of organizations, and we believe that these uses will be valuable to public- and private-sector entities, independent of the entity size (e.g., both large and small).

Auditing Mechanism

The sunburst visualization of the cyberdefensive strategies facilitates the ability to easily assess how cyberdefensive resources are being allocated within an organization. This was a key motivation behind our work for DHS CFO/PA&E, given its role in determining program effectiveness. A programming office that records resource allocation for cyberdefensive actions (e.g., the budget expended toward actions such as generating rapid response plans versus the absence of a budget allocated to other actions, such as developing tools for testing isolation) can review these allocations and visually depict how the resources are distributed across the set of possible actions. The visualizations allow for quickly determining over-expensed and under-expensed actions, as well as other misalignments of spending in a way that can be communicated across multiple management layers of a large organization.

Some challenges will exist in the auditing process, such as the ability to compare actions that are difficult to quantify along the same dimension. For example, the action of "minimizing exposure" may not necessarily be associated with a financial quantity, while actions such as "block cyberattacks" (e.g., through firewalls) are readily associated with financial amounts. For this reason, a suitable approach for quantifying all actions will be necessary depending on the selected auditing mechanism.

Prescriptive Mechanism

The cyberdefensive organization presented herein can be used when developing a cyberdefensive strategy. The actions described in this work are presented in a top-down hierarchy that can be used to guide a CISO in identifying appropriate cyberdefensive actions for a given organization's needs. It should be noted that many of the actions presented in the preceding pages are not universally applicable to all organizations and should be adopted on an as-needed basis. For example, it is likely that the strategy of increasing resilience should be prioritized over accelerating recovery in the case of organizations that provide services for medical emergencies (e.g., critical infrastructure for first responders), since increasing resilience focuses on preventing interruptions, whereas accelerating recovery assumes that a system will go down (though, hopefully for a short period of time). Other organizations that can withstand downtime may consider accelerating recovery a key component of their strategy. Similarly, some organizations may choose to emphasize minimizing unnecessary exposure as a key strategy (especially if the convenience of network-accessibility is not a highly valued benefit), while other organizations may not be able to feasibly engage in this strategy, as it may go against the organization's raison d'être. For organizations evaluating the "minimize exposure" strategy, we recommend that careful thought be given to the costs and benefits of web accessibility for each class of the organization's information for which network exposure is being considered.

Improving the Cyberdefensive Actions

As mentioned previously, the cyberdefensive actions presented in this report represent an iterative process of selection and review, though this process did not incorporate consideration for explicit resource allocation. We believe the actions are largely accurate, though we acknowledge that there is likely room for improving some components of the presented actions to arrive at a customized set of actions based on an organization's characteristics. We can think of the presented actions as an enumeration (a hierarchical list of actions) with an implicit calibration that is indicated by the angles of the sunburst wedges (a prioritization or allocation strategy among the actions based on respective wedge sizes). As implied in the preceding section, the specific enumeration and calibration will vary across organizations, in that the space of actions will differ by organization (two organizations will generally not share identical enumerations) and the relative importance of the various actions will vary across organizations (two organizations that share an enumeration may have differing priorities).

To develop the cyberdefensive actions that are appropriate for a given organization, we recommend a process that iterates between measuring actual cyber resource allocation and subsequent modification of prescriptive resource allocation. The measurement phase should involve quantifying the actual allocation of cyber resources, including personnel and financial resources. In essence, this phase would generate a sunburst diagram based on current resources. In addition to measuring allocated resources, this phase should include a measure of unwanted cyber activity (e.g., attack attempts, successful attacks, losses incurred) over a designated period of time. In the modification phase, changes to the allocation of resources should be made. This may involve deemphasizing and/or expanding actions and adding/removing other actions, as appropriate. Upon completion of the modification phase, the measurement phase should be repeated, and the process should continue to iterate accordingly. This approach can serve as a useful mechanism for optimizing the cyberdefensive strategy of a given organization.

Applying the Model to Broader IT Compliance Efforts

An additional benefit of this model may be found in other domains involving complex IT policy compliance that is not necessarily cybersecurity-based. For example, Sarbanes Oxley, Federal Information Security Management Act (FISMA), and Payment Card Industry Data Security Standard (PCI/DSS) compliance involves many complex steps that often overwhelm participants within the private sector and federal government. Using an approach similar to that contained herein may simplify the process of compliance. For example, Sarbanes Oxley consists of 11 major elements, including Auditor Independence (Title II), Corporate Responsibility (Title III) and White Collar Crime Penalty Enhancement (Title IX). Each of these, in turn, involves a complex set of activities to ensure compliance. The Cyber Sunburst Graph we have presented in this report can be applied to this set of activities, to enable clarity and allow for prioritization by a team engaged in Sarbanes Oxley compliance.

CHAPTER SIX

Conclusion

Developing a cyberdefense strategy requires selecting defensive and preventative activities from a large set of possible actions. This selection process is difficult because there is no way to guarantee that a strategy is sufficient to defend against an attack, but, as additional actions are added to a strategy, the total cost of fulfilling the strategy increases nonlinearly. The result is that a strategy must be judiciously determined with an eye toward both effectiveness and practicality, especially given that this process typically occurs in the context of limited resources.

We believe that recognizing the interrelationships among the possible actions can facilitate the selection process and provide a basis by which a practitioner can allocate and prioritize actions according to the dependencies among them. In this regard, we hierarchically organized cyberdefensive actions according to their relationships. If two actions are directly related, we characterize the relationship as being one of two possible types of relationships: composition or requisition. In a composition relationship, the parent (or general) action is an aggregation of two or more child (or specific) actions (e.g., a meal is composed of a salad, soup, main course, and dessert). In a requisition relationship, one or more child (specific) actions must be completed (are *required*) before the parent (or general) action can complete (e.g., a meal requires buying, cooking, and serving food). We illustrated the total set of related actions with a sunburst diagram.

This approach to considering cyberdefensive activities is intended to aid CISOs and their support teams in taking a circumspect view of an organization's cyberdefense strategy. As resources are moved between different components of a cyberdefense strategy, the approach presented herein should enable a transparent view of the associated costs in terms of money, time and otherwise. We believe that an extension of this approach may also facilitate a quantifiable understanding of the relative benefits of the cyber actions contained within a strategy. Moreover, by applying this methodology across a set of organizations (say, within the same sector, across different sectors, or across different government agencies), a good deal of information could be learned about best/common practices, outlier organizations, or actions that are either under- or over-addressed.

References

Ablon, Lillian, Martin C. Libicki, and Andrea A. Golay, *Markets for Cybercrime Tools and Stolen Data: Hackers' Bazaar*, Santa Monica, Calif.: RAND Corporation, RR-610-JNI, 2014. As of October 7, 2015:
http://www.rand.org/pubs/research_reports/RR610.html

Banjo, Shelly, "Home Depot Hackers Exposed 53 Million Email Addresses," *Wall Street Journal*, November 6, 2015. As of October 7, 2015:
http://www.wsj.com/articles/home-depot-hackers-used-password-stolen-from-vendor-1415309282

Christey, Steve, ed., *2011 CWE/SANS Top 25 Most Dangerous Software Errors*, The MITRE Corporation, September 13, 2011. As of October 7, 2015:
http://cwe.mitre.org/top25/

Cisco Systems, Inc., "Disaster Recovery: Best Practices," white paper, 2008. As of October 7, 2015:
http://www.cisco.com/en/US/technologies/collateral/tk869/tk769/white_paper_c11-453495.html

Constantin, Lucian, "Attackers Use NTP Reflection in Huge DDoS Attack," *ComputerWorld.com*, February 11, 2014. As of October 7, 2015:
http://www.computerworld.com/article/2487573/
network-security/attackers-use-ntp-reflection-in-huge-ddos-attack.html

Defense Information Systems Agency, "HBSS," undated. As of October 7, 2015:
http://www.disa.mil/Services/Cybersecurity/HBSS

"Depth First vs. Breadth First," Github.com, 2012. As of October 7, 2015:
https://github.com/tinkerpop/gremlin/wiki/Depth-First-vs.-Breadth-First

DHS Blueprint—*See* U.S. Department of Homeland Security, *Blueprint for a Secure Cyber Future: The Cybersecurity Strategy for the Homeland Security Enterprise.*

Federal Energy Regulatory Commission and North American Electric Reliability Corporation, *Arizona-Southern California Outages on September 8, 2011: Causes and Recommendations*, April 2012. As of October 7, 2015:
https://www.ferc.gov/legal/staff-reports/04-27-2012-ferc-nerc-report.pdf

Finifter, Matthew, Devdatta Akhawe, and David Wagner, "An Empirical Study of Vulnerability Rewards Programs," presented at USENIX Security Symposium, August 15, 2013. As of October 7, 2015:
http://0b4af6cdc2f0c5998459-c0245c5c937c5dedcca3f1764ecc9b2f.r43.cf2.rackcdn.com/12309-sec13-paper_finifter.pdf

Geer, Daniel, Rebecca Bace, Peter Gutmann, Perry Metzger, Charles P. Pfleeger, John S. Quarterman, and Bruce Schneier, "Cyber*In*security: The Cost of Monopoly," *Computer and Communications Industry Association Report*, September 2003.

Ginter, Andrew, "13 Ways Your Firewall Could Fail You," Wired.com Innovation Insights blog, August 12, 2013. As of October 7, 2015:
http://insights.wired.com/profiles/blogs/do-you-know-the-13-ways-your-firewall-could-fail-you#axzz3BVmKYKBs

Goodin, Dan, "AWS Console Breach Leads to Demise of Service with 'Proven' Backup Plan," *ArsTechnica.com*, June 18, 2014. As of October 7, 2015:
http://arstechnica.com/security/2014/06/
aws-console-breach-leads-to-demise-of-service-with-proven-backup-plan/

Hughes, David, "Brighton Bombing: Daily Telegraph Journalist Recalls," *The Telegraph,* October 11, 2009. As of October 7, 2015:
http://www.telegraph.co.uk/news/politics/6300215/Brighton-bombing-Daily-Telegraph-journalist-recalls.html

Kaiser, Tiffany, "Target Missed Early Warning Signs of Holiday Data Breach," *DailyTech.com,* March 13, 2014. As of October 7, 2015:
http://www.dailytech.com/Target+Missed+Early+Warning+Signs+of+Holiday+Data+Breach/article34518.htm

Keizer, Gregg, "Best Buy Sold Infected Digital Picture Frames," *Computerworld.com*, January 23, 2008. As of October 7, 2015:
http://www.computerworld.com/s/article/9058638/Best_Buy_sold_infected_digital_picture_frames

Kent, Glenn A., and David Ochmanek, *A Framework for Modernization Within the United States Air Force*, Santa Monica, Calif.: RAND Corporation, MR-1706-AF, 2003. As of October 7, 2015:
http://www.rand.org/pubs/monograph_reports/MR1706.html

Krebs, Brian, "Email Attack on Vendor Set Up Breach at Target," KrebsOnSecurity.com blog, February 12, 2014. As of October 7, 2015:
http://krebsonsecurity.com/2014/02/email-attack-on-vendor-set-up-breach-at-target/

———, "Rustock Botnet Flatlined, Spam Volumes Plummet," KrebsOnSecurity.com blog, March 16, 2011. As of October 7, 2015:
http://krebsonsecurity.com/2011/03/rustock-botnet-flatlined-spam-volumes-plummet/

———, "Security Fix for Critical Java Flaw Released," KrebsOnSecurity.com blog, August 30, 2012. As of October 7, 2015:
http://krebsonsecurity.com/2012/08/security-fix-for-critical-java-flaw-released/

Lemos, Robert, "NSA Attempting to Design Crack-Proof Computer," *ZDNet.com*, February 1, 2001. As of October 7, 2015:
http://www.zdnet.com/news/nsa-attempting-to-design-crack-proof-computer/114035

Libicki, Martin C., David Senty, and Julia Pollak, *Hackers Wanted: An Examination of the Cybersecurity Labor Market*, Santa Monica, Calif.: RAND Corporation, RR-430, 2014. As of October 7, 2015:
http://www.rand.org/pubs/research_reports/RR430.html

Lord, Timothy, "iPhone Hacked in Under 60 Seconds Using Malicious Charger," Slashdot.com blog, August 2, 2013. As of October 7, 2015:
http://apple-beta.slashdot.org/story/13/08/01/2024212/
iphone-hacked-in-under-60-seconds-using-malicious-charger

Mimoso, Michael, "Hackers Using Brute-Force Attacks to Harvest WordPress Sites," *ThreatPost.com,* April 15, 2013. As of October 7, 2015:
http://threatpost.com/hackers-using-brute-force-attacks-harvest-wordpress-sites-041513/77730

The MITRE Corporation, "Common Weakness Enumeration," 2014. As of October 7, 2015:
http://cwe.mitre.org/

Moore, Jack, "White House Cyber Czar's Goal: 'Kill the Password Dead,'" FederalNewsRadio.com, June 18, 2014. As of October 7, 2015:
http://www.federalnewsradio.com/241/3646015/White-House-cyber-czars-goal-Kill-the-password-dead

Moscaritolo, Angela, "RSA Confirms Lockheed Hack Linked to SecurID Breach," *SC Magazine,* June 7, 2011. As of October 7, 2015:
http://www.scmagazine.com/rsa-confirms-lockheed-hack-linked-to-securid-breach/article/204744/

Nakashima, Ellen, "Pentagon Cyber Unit Wants to 'Get Inside the Bad Guy's Head,'" *Washington Post*, June 19, 2014. As of October 7, 2015:
http://www.washingtonpost.com/news/checkpoint/wp/2014/06/19/
pentagon-cyber-unit-wants-to-get-inside-the-bad-guys-head/

National Research Council, *Professionalizing the Nation's Cybersecurity Workforce? Criteria for Decision-Making*, Washington, D.C.: National Academies Press, 2013.

Osborne, Charlie, "Georgia Turns the Tables on Russian Hacker," *ZDNet.com*, October 30, 2012. As of October 7, 2015:
http://www.zdnet.com/georgia-turns-the-tables-on-russian-hacker-7000006611/

Partnership for Disaster Resilience, *Post-Disaster Recovery Planning Forum: How-To Guide*, 2007. As of October 7, 2015:
http://nws.weather.gov/nthmp/Minutes/oct-nov07/post-disaster_recovery_planning_forum_uo-csc-2.pdf

Perrin, Chad, "The CIA Triad," TechRepublic.com blog, June 30, 2008. As of October 7, 2015:
http://www.techrepublic.com/blog/it-security/the-cia-triad/

Perrow, Charles, *Normal Accidents: Living with High-Risk Technologies*, 2nd edition, New York: Basic Books, 1984.

Rogers, Mike, and C.A. Dutch Ruppersberger, *Investigative Report on the U.S. National Security Issues Posed by Chinese Telecommunications Companies Huawei and ZTE*, Washington, D.C.: U.S. House of Representatives, October 8, 2012. As of October 7, 2015:
https://intelligence.house.gov/sites/intelligence.house.gov/files/documents/
Huawei-ZTE%20Investigative%20Report%20%28FINAL%29.pdf

Saltzer, J. H., and M. D. Schroeder, "The Protection of Information in Computer Systems," *Proceedings of the IEEE*, Vol. 63, No. 9, September 1975, pp. 1278–1308.

Sanger, David E., and Thom Shanker, "N.S.A. Devises Radio Pathway into Computers," *New York Times*, January 14, 2014. As of October 7, 2015:
http://www.nytimes.com/2014/01/15/us/nsa-effort-pries-open-computers-not-connected-to-internet.html

Smith, Josh, "Homeland Security Official: Some Foreign-Made Electronics Compromise Cybersecurity," *NationalJournal.com*, July 7, 2011.

Symantec Corporation, *Internet Security Threat Report 2013*, Volume 18, Mountain View, Calif., April 2013. As of October 7, 2015:
http://www.symantec.com/content/en/us/enterprise/other_resources/b-istr_main_report_
v18_2012_21291018.en-us.pdf

Thaler, David E., *Strategies to Tasks: A Framework for Linking Means and Ends*, Santa Monica, Calif.: RAND Corporation, MR-300-AF, 1993. As of October 7, 2015:
http://www.rand.org/pubs/monograph_reports/MR300.html

"Transcript of President Obama's Jan. 17 Speech on NSA Reforms," *Washington Post*, January 17, 2014. As of October 7, 2015:
http://www.washingtonpost.com/politics/full-text-of-president-obamas-jan-17-speech-on-nsa-
reforms/2014/01/17/fa33590a-7f8c-11e3-9556-4a4bf7bcbd84_story.html

Trivedi, Kishor S., Dong Seong Kim, and Rahul Ghosh, "Resilience in Computer Systems and Networks," presented at 2009 IEEE/ACM International Conference on Computer-Aided Design Digest of Technical Papers, November 2009. As of October 7, 2015:
http://ieeexplore.ieee.org/xpl/articleDetails.jsp?arnumber=5361311&filter%3DAND%
28p_IS_Number%3A5361202%29

Urbina, Ian, "Hacker Tactic: Holding Data Hostage," *New York Times*, June 21, 2014. As of October 7, 2015:
http://www.nytimes.com/2014/06/22/sunday-review/hackers-find-new-ways-to-breach-computer-security.html

U.S. Department of Commerce, National Institute of Standards and Technology, *Security and Privacy Controls for Federal Information Systems and Organizations*, Special Publication 800-53, 2013.

U.S. Department of Energy, *21 Steps to Improve Cyber Security of SCADA Networks*, 2009. As of October 7, 2015:
http://energy.gov/sites/prod/files/oeprod/DocumentsandMedia/21_Steps_-_SCADA.pdf

U.S. Department of Homeland Security, *Blueprint for a Secure Cyber Future: The Cybersecurity Strategy for the Homeland Security Enterprise*, Washington, D.C., 2014. As of October 7, 2015:
http://www.dhs.gov/blueprint-secure-cyber-future

———, *The 2014 Quadrennial Homeland Security Review*, Washington, D.C., 2014.

The White House, *Comprehensive National Cybersecurity Initiative*, 2009. As of October 22, 2015:
https://www.whitehouse.gov/issues/foreign-policy/cybersecurity/national-initiative

Yee, Ka-Ping, "User Interaction Design for Secure Systems," in *Proceedings of the 4th International Conference on Information and Communications Security*, R. Deng et al., eds., LNCS 2513, Springer, 2002, pp. 278–290.

Zetter, Kim, "Pentagon Hacker McKinnon Wins 10-Year Extradition Battle," *Wired.com*, October 16, 2012. As of October 7, 2015:
http://www.wired.com/2012/10/mckinnon-extradition-win/